The Hidden History
of American
Healthcare

THE

HIDDEN HISTORY *of*
AMERICAN
HEALTHCARE

WHY SICKNESS
BANKRUPTS YOU
AND MAKES OTHERS
INSANELY RICH

THOM HARTMANN

BK

Berrett–Koehler Publishers, Inc.

Berrett-Koehler Publishers, Inc.
1333 Broadway, Suite 1000
Oakland, CA 94612-1921
Tel: (510) 817-2277
Fax: (510) 817-2278
www.bkconnection.com

ORDERING INFORMATION
Quantity sales. Special discounts are available on quantity purchases by corporations, associations, and others. For details, contact the "Special Sales Department" at the Berrett-Koehler address above.
Individual sales. Berrett-Koehler publications are available through most bookstores. They can also be ordered directly from Berrett-Koehler: Tel: (800) 929-2929; Fax: (802) 864-7626; www.bkconnection.com.
Orders for college textbook / course adoption use. Please contact Berrett-Koehler: Tel: (800) 929-2929; Fax: (802) 864-7626.

Distributed to the U.S. trade and internationally by Penguin Random House Publisher Services.

Berrett-Koehler and the BK logo are registered trademarks of Berrett-Koehler Publishers, Inc.

Printed in the United States of America

Berrett-Koehler books are printed on long-lasting acid-free paper. When it is available, we choose paper that has been manufactured by environmentally responsible processes. These may include using trees grown in sustainable forests, incorporating recycled paper, minimizing chlorine in bleaching, or recycling the energy produced at the paper mill.

Library of Congress Cataloging-in-Publication Data
Name: Hartmann, Thom, 1951– author.
Title: The hidden history of American healthcare : why sickness bankrupts you and makes others insanely rich / Thom Hartmann.
Description: First edition. | Oakland, CA : Berrett-Koehler Publishers,bInc., [2021] | Series: The Thom Hartmann hidden history series; 5 | Includes bibliographical references and index.
Identifiers: LCCN 2021013081 | ISBN 9781523091638 (paperback) | ISBN 9781523091645 (adobe pdf) | ISBN 9781523091652 (epub)
Subjects: LCSH: Medical care—United States. | Medical care, Cost of—United States. | Consumer education—United States.
Classification: LCC RA410.53 .H372 2021 | DDC 362.10973—dc23
LC record available at https://lccn.loc.gov/2021013081

First Edition
27 26 25 24 23 22 21

10 9 8 7 6 5 4 3 2 1

Book production: Linda Jupiter Productions
Interior design: Good Morning Graphics
Proofread: Mary Kanable

Cover design: Wes Youssi, M.80 Design
Edit: Elissa Rabellino
Index: Paula C. Durbin-Westby

To our children, Kindra, Justin, and Kerith,
who make their parents so proud by
(among other things) all working in public health.

*We pledge ourselves to work unceasingly in State and Nation
for . . . [t]he protection of home life against the hazards
of sickness, irregular employment, and old age through the
adoption of a system of social insurance adapted to American use.*

*What Germany has done in the way of old age pensions
or insurance should be studied by us, and the system adapted
to our uses, with whatever modifications are rendered necessary
by our different ways of life and habits of thought.*

–Theodore Roosevelt, 1912

CONTENTS

How a Single-Payer Healthcare System Helped Stop COVID-19

Healthcare systems can also be national security systems. Just ask anyone from Taiwan.

On January 20, 2020, the United States recorded its first known case of COVID-19 infection. The following day, Taiwan got their first, too.

By the end of April, over a million Americans were infected with the virus,[1] but Taiwan had recorded only 388 infections and their last case of local transmission on April 12. (A few had arrived on aircraft from other countries; all were contained by quarantine.)[2]

As of this writing in September 2020, there hadn't been a single new case or a single death in Taiwan since April. The economy never shut down and, at this writing, was projected to have grown nearly 2 percent in 2020; business, restaurants, theaters, and sports events were all open. Life was back to normal (albeit a mask-wearing normal).

And it was made possible by their national single-payer healthcare system and their citizens' willingness to do their bit for the collective good.

Back in the 1980s, Taiwan was on the edge of moving toward a democracy (after a military coup in the 1960s), and about 40 percent of Taiwanese people didn't have health insurance. If somebody in a family got sick, the cost of care often wiped out the family, and demands for reform were loud across the nation.

Uwe Reinhardt was a German-born healthcare economist married to a Taiwanese woman, and he attended a conference on healthcare in Taipei in 1989. His presentation impressed representatives of the government in attendance, and while he was still in town for the conference, they asked him for his best suggestion for a national healthcare system.

He and his wife went back to their hotel and discussed the issue in depth, finally deciding that a single-payer national system would be the most cost-effective, efficient, and comprehensive program possible. He shared his thoughts with the government representatives, and the next day he left Taiwan to go back to Princeton, where he was an economics professor.

Six months later, a representative of Taiwan's government called him to say that they were going to take up his suggestion and asked him to help them craft their program. He enthusiastically assented, and by 1995 Taiwan had instituted one of the world's best systems.[3]

Today, everybody in Taiwan is fully covered for doctor and hospital services. Everybody has a driver's-license-like healthcare card, which accesses their entire medical history. They can book a doctor's appointment on any computer terminal in the country, and the entire cost of the system is a bit more than

6 percent of Taiwan's GDP (in the United States, healthcare consumes 24 percent of our GDP) because there are no insurance company intermediaries sucking profits off the system.

When COVID-19 hit, Taiwan chose not to use the blunt-force technique of shutting down their economy and locking people in. Instead, they took on the coronavirus with an aggressive, nationwide test-and-contact-trace program tied in to the national health service database. Every infected person was identified and put into a comfortable quarantine, and every person he or she had come into contact with—even very marginal contacts—was also tested and their contacts traced.

By April, just a bit more than two months after their first case surfaced, the country had the coronavirus isolated and completely under control. By quarantining inbound visitors to the island nation of 23 million, they were able (as of this writing) to keep it that way.

Maintaining public health is one of the most important functions of any nation's healthcare system. Because America's is so fragmented, it's inconceivable that our nation could respond to an epidemic, a pandemic, or another public health disaster with the speed and elegance of Taiwan or any of the world's other nations with single-payer Medicare for All types of systems.

Medicare for All–Why?

"It's like Stockholm Syndrome," a friend who's a psychotherapist said, describing the way that Americans have clung, for more than five generations, to for-profit health insurance while the rest of the world figured out how to provide healthcare to all citizens at a much lower price. "People know it and have become familiar with it," she added. "They can't imagine anything else."

It's probably the largest con job ever perpetrated on the American people, one that has cost trillions of dollars and millions of lives. It's been going on since the 1940s.

If it were a scientific experiment, it would have been shut down by the ethics review panels generations ago. This experiment in providing healthcare via a for-profit insurance system has led to the deaths of more Americans than we lost in World War II.[4]

Every year, over a half million Americans go bankrupt—often losing pretty much everything they've worked their entire lives for—because someone in their family got sick. That's a half million families a year, every year, for the past few decades.[5] And the coronavirus has only made things worse.

Perhaps most galling, this massive rip-off is costing our entire nation—and each of us individually—a fortune.

Insurance premiums right now make up 22 percent of all taxable payroll, well above what the cost of Medicare for All would be, at around 14 percent when first put into place, dropping to around 10 percent within a few years as previously uninsured people get their health needs up to date.

As the health insurance, drug, and hospital parasites pushed their suckers deeper and deeper into our body politic, spending on healthcare by Americans went up 25 percent between 2007 and 2014 at the same time that spending on housing, food, and clothing fell by 6, 8, and 19 percent, respectively.[6]

In 2018 alone, the United States wasted $256 billion on "administrative expenses" associated with for-profit health insurance, including multimillion-dollar salaries and armies of bean counters who scour claims looking for reasons to reject payment of hospital, doctor, and pharmaceutical bills.[7]

American doctors and hospitals employ eight times as many people as doctors and hospitals in Canada for administration, with US doctors spending 12 percent of their total billings just on the hassle of getting reimbursed.[8]

My physician, when we lived in Washington, DC, told me about a colleague of hers who specializes in liver disease. Because the new hepatitis C drugs cost tens of thousands of dollars and the for-profit health insurance companies fight paying for them, he has two full-time nurses on staff whose only job is to constantly rebill and fight with the insurance companies so that his patients can get the therapy.

And because big drug companies charge Americans, on average, about twice what they charge Canadians or citizens of any other developed country, we pay them another roughly $200 billion a year that all goes to executive salaries and into the pockets of the investor class.

Lawrence O'Donnell told author Kurt Andersen about how, when he was an aide to Senator Daniel Patrick Moynihan back in the last century, the storied senator asked him, "Why don't we just delete the words 'age 65' from the Medicare statute?"

This question, O'Donnell told Andersen, followed "twenty-four hearings studying every detail of healthcare policy." O'Donnell noted that Moynihan "hated unnecessary government complexity."[9]

The United States has been engaged in a 70-year-long experiment to determine whether it's ever possible for healthcare to be provided purely on a for-profit basis in a way that maximizes efficiency, fairness, and optimal outcomes.

We've proved that it's not possible. And the experiment has been disastrous for Americans—particularly Americans of color—in terms of cost, lives lost, and overall quality of life.

If the goal of a healthcare system is to extend life and improve the quality of health, we have totally failed. Citizens of every other developed democracy have a longer life span and better health outcomes than we do, and none of them spend even half as much per person on healthcare as we do.

The only area where we've done well is with people over 65, and that is entirely because of our government-administered program, Medicare.

People on Medicare live as long as in other countries with national healthcare systems, while younger Americans relying on the for-profit insurance system are more likely to die.

But to the insurance industry it's all just math and numbers; it's as if the lives of Americans are irrelevant.

For example, the *medical loss ratio* (MLR) is the percentage of an insurance company's income from premiums that's paid out for actual care. In the US insurance system it's around 80 percent, with the remaining 20 percent of its trillions in annual revenues going to profits and huge executive salaries.

With Medicare in the United States and similar systems in pretty much every other developed country in the world, the MLR is between 95 and 98 percent, depending on how you calculate overhead costs. Nothing goes to profits, and overhead is minimal (on both the insurance side and the hospital/doctor side) because there's only one single payer to keep track of.

Health insurance companies use two systems to keep the MLR as low as possible to keep profits as high as possible: *cherry picking* and *lemon dropping*.

Cherry picking refers to offering policies that appeal to young, healthy people (with perks like gym memberships and with high deductibles and low costs); lemon dropping describes ways to discourage or outright reject people who may be expensive—mostly people who are obese, smokers, diabetics, and older adults—through configuring plans and coverage to avoid insuring such folks.

While every insurance company and most for-profit hospitals in America run these schemes every day, they don't exist in other developed nations.

But here in America, an estimated $500 billion to over $1 trillion a year is skimmed off the top of our healthcare system by for-profit hospitals, Big Pharma, for-profit insurance companies, and all the various benefits managers and other leeches on the back of our system.

Even the supposedly nonprofit segments of the US healthcare system are massively corrupt. A 2019 *Forbes* article appropriately titled "Top US 'Non-Profit' Hospitals & CEOs Are Racking Up Huge Profits" reported, "Collectively, $297.5 million in cash compensation flowed to the top paid executive at each of the [nation's largest] 82 [nonprofit] hospitals. We found payouts as high as $10 million, $18 million and even $21.6 million per CEO or other top-paid employee."[10]

The average American is paying as much as $3,000 a year more than Canadians or Europeans just in healthcare expenses, as this cash is transferred from mostly working-class Americans to the billionaires and multimillionaires who run and/or own stock in our for-profit system.[11]

Medicare for All—How?

When Robert Ball worked with President Lyndon Johnson to develop our modern Medicare system, he explicitly did so in a way that would allow it to be quickly transformed from a program for the elderly into a universal healthcare system. All that would be necessary, he said of his initial design, would be to do away with the "over 65" age requirement and add in new funding measures (or just pull more from the general fund).

GUT THE GAP

That plan got somewhat blown up when Republicans and Southern Democrats insisted that people must have "skin in the game" to avoid "abuse" of the system and, when Medicare was passed in 1965, inserted a 20 percent gap in coverage that people would have to fill out of their own pockets.

Although the record of debate on the issue is shockingly thin, there are two obvious reasons why this coalition would favor the "gap" in Medicare coverage.

For the Republicans and "conservative" (corporate-owned) Democrats, that gap represented a multibillion-dollar profit opportunity for insurance companies to expand into; and expand they did, with Medigap policies now covering over

14 million Americans. Tragically, that's only a bit more than a third of all Medicare beneficiaries; most elderly people can't afford the additional $150–$500 a month for a Medigap policy and thus can end up on the hook for 20 percent of an *unlimited* expense if they get seriously ill.[12]

For the Southern Democrats, there was another benefit to the gap. The GOP was then in the early stages of what came to be called Nixon's "Southern Strategy" of picking up the white racist vote from Democrats following LBJ's signing of the Civil Rights and Voting Rights Acts in 1964–1965, and white racism was the most potent force that kept these politicians in power in the South. Imposing a 20 percent copay on Medicare expenses pretty much guaranteed that poor Black people would avoid medical care for anything except a life-or-death emergency.

There was one major addition to Medicare, in 1972, when the program was expanded during the Nixon administration to include Social Security Disability Insurance (SSDI), which covers medical costs for disabled people under 65, but it keeps the gap, so even younger disabled people must buy Medigap insurance if they can afford it.[13]

For a Medicare for All program to truly work as it does in most other developed countries, we must get rid of the gap.

BUILD A ROBUST SYSTEM

A study by Johns Hopkins found that the United States has 19 percent fewer doctors, 26 percent fewer acute care hospital beds, and 25 percent fewer nurses than the average for developed countries across the world.

"Similarly," they said, "the U.S. in 2015 had only 7.5 new medical school graduates per 100,000 population, compared to the OECD median of 12.1, and just 2.5 acute care hospital beds per 1,000 population compared to the OECD median of 3.4."[14]

A *JAMA* study found that "[t]he U.S. remains an outlier in terms of per capita healthcare spending, which was $9,892 in 2016," and that was "about 25 percent higher than second-place Switzerland's $7,919."

Switzerland, though, has the most expensive healthcare system in the world (it's not a single-payer system—everybody must buy insurance, although all the systems are nonprofit). Looking at the rest of the world, *JAMA* pointed out that our $9,892 per person "was also 108 percent higher than Canada's $4,753, and 145 percent higher than the Organization for Economic Cooperation and Development (OECD) median of $4,033."[15]

In the face of all this, fully one out of every 10 Americans has *no* health insurance coverage of any sort—government, private, or otherwise—and this is almost a decade after full implementation of the Affordable Care Act and its attendant expansion of Medicaid.[16]

The *JAMA* study looked at 10 countries (United Kingdom, Canada, Germany, Australia, Japan, Sweden, France, the Netherlands, Switzerland, and Denmark) in addition to the United States. For every 1,000 babies born in America, 5.8 die in infancy; the average for the rest of these countries (including the United States) is 3.6.

The same 2016 study showed that the average life expectancy in the rest of the countries ranged from 80.7 years to

83.9 years, but here in the United States, with a clunky healthcare system and a collection of parasitic health insurance companies attached to our backs, people only lived to an average age of 78.8.[17] The US life expectancy fell by an additional entire year to 77.8 in 2020 because of the disastrous way the Trump administration handed the COVID-19 pandemic.[18]

We're also the least healthy in the developed world. The *JAMA* study found that while obesity and "severe overweight" rates ranged from 23.8 to 63.4 percent of the other 10 nations' populations, it's 70.1 percent here.

In those countries where everybody pays into a single system, there are both government and socially based incentives to encourage healthy eating and other practices to save taxpayers money. In our nation, huge profits in the food industry, which constitutes around 5 percent of GDP, drive advertising and consumption, while there are no government campaigns to either rein in or actively discourage consumption of obesity- causing food products.[19]

It's truly extraordinary how rapidly America's health has deteriorated, and big money and politics are at the root of much of it.

PART ONE

How Bad Things Are in America

How the Insurance Industry Bought Joe Lieberman and Killed the Public Option

Want to deny affordable health insurance to millions, leading to thousands of unnecessary and/or early deaths, all in order to keep your profits high? Just hand Joe Lieberman $1,182,070 over the course of his political career and you own the guy. He'll make sure to kill a public option, all with a smile.[1]

As Paul Begala wrote of the time Lieberman killed the Obamacare public option, "Connecticut Senator Joe Lieberman is identified as (I-CT). But the 'I' does not stand for 'Independent.' It stands for 'Insurance Industry.'"[2]

New York Times staff writer David E. Rosenbaum reported, about a previous Lieberman pro-insurance-industry action in 2000, "Many of Mr. Lieberman's friends said he had no alternative but to take this position because it was the one favored by the insurance industry. The industry is important to Connecticut's economy and has generously donated to Mr. Lieberman's campaigns over the years."[3]

And, of course, it's not just Joe Lieberman. Every single Republican in both the US House and Senate voted against President Barack Obama's plan to provide affordable health insurance to every American, and odds are, every single one of them was well rewarded for the effort.

That said, the Affordable Care Act was always an unnecessarily complex Rube Goldberg effort.

President Obama and his Democratic colleagues knew that if they tried to offer the American public any sort of nonprofit or Medicare for All health coverage, the trillion-dollar for-profit insurance, hospital, and pharmaceutical industries would unleash a scorched-earth campaign against them, from which many would never politically recover.

Conservatives on the US Supreme Court in 1976, 1978, and 2010 radically rewrote American campaign finance law to give billionaires and large, powerful industries political life-and-death power over even the most august of politicians.[4]

Ever since Senator Bernie Sanders of Vermont raised the profile of Medicare for All, dozens of Democratic politicians have candidly said, some to me in private and a few in public, that it would be a great thing for the American people, would save hundreds of billions of dollars a year, and would save lives . . . but can't pass because it's "politically impossible."

That's code for our elected representatives lacking the power to overcome multimillion-dollar pressure campaigns launched by well-funded and highly profitable corporations and the think tanks and media organizations that also take their money.

As a result, any sort of reform that didn't increase profits for the largest industries—particularly the health insurance industry—was doomed to fail, at least during normal times. Thus, President Obama took the plan that the Heritage Foundation, a conservative think tank, had put together in the 1980s,[5] which Mitt Romney put into place as governor of Massachusetts in 2006.[6]

It was an improvement on the status quo, but only a slight one.

Obamacare: Rube Goldberg
Meets Health Insurance

As with most politicians interested in producing the best healthcare outcomes for the nation at the lowest cost, there was a time in his political career that Illinois state senator Barack Obama was an outspoken advocate for a national single-payer Medicare for All type of health insurance system like Canada's.

"I happen to be a proponent of a single-payer universal healthcare program," Obama said in a June 30, 2003, speech.

"I see no reason," he added, "why the United States of America, the wealthiest country in the history of the world, spending 14 percent of its gross national product on healthcare, cannot provide basic health insurance to everybody. And that's what Jim is talking about when he says everybody in, nobody out. A single-payer healthcare plan, a universal healthcare plan. That's what I'd like to see."[7]

By the time he was running for president in 2008, his need for campaign cash from wealthy corporate-related donors had grown and his thoughts had "evolved."

"What are not legitimate concerns are those being put forward claiming a public option is somehow a Trojan horse for a single-payer system," Obama told the American Medical Association on June 15, 2009, half a year into his first term.

"I'll be honest," he said. "There are countries where a single-payer system may be working. But I believe—and I've even taken some flak from members of my own party for this belief—that it is important for us to build on our traditions here in the United States. So, when you hear the naysayers claim that I'm trying to bring about government-run health-care, know this—they are not telling the truth."[8]

Instead of Medicare for All, Obama suggested what 2016 Democratic presidential candidate Pete Buttigieg called "Medicare for Anybody Who Wants It," also known as the "public option."

Additionally, he suggested expanding Medicaid and having the state governments administer health insurance portals to make buying for-profit health insurance more convenient (since he was going to require everybody in the country not covered by Medicaid to purchase this product), along with government-funded subsidies for part of the premium costs.

The federal government subsidies would have the effect of keeping the multibillion-dollar profits of the for-profit health insurance companies high, while not inflicting the entire expense on taxpayers/consumers.

He campaigned for president in 2008 on what came to be known as Obamacare or, more properly, the Affordable Care Act, and the public Medicare option part of his plan brought along enough of the progressive Democratic base that this virtually unknown Midwestern politician was able to defeat the massively funded and establishment-supported Clinton machine to take the Democratic nomination and then the White House.

Even half a year into his first term, President Obama continued to promote the idea of everybody in America being able to choose to purchase Medicare instead of a for-profit plan from one of the giant insurance corporations.

On July 18, 2009, for example, he said, "Any plan I sign must include an insurance exchange—a one-stop-shopping marketplace where you can compare the benefits, costs and track records of a variety of plans, including a public option to increase competition and keep insurance companies honest."[9]

House Speaker Nancy Pelosi was totally behind the public option and even brought former Aetna insurance industry executive Wendell Potter to testify before Congress on its behalf. He wrote in 2015,

> *In an effort to keep the public option idea alive, House Speaker Nancy Pelosi invited me to testify during a Sept. 16, 2009, meeting of the Democratic Steering and Policy Committee Forum on Health Insurance Reform.*
>
> *Knowing the industry as I did, I told the committee that if Congress failed to create a public option to compete with private insurers, "the bill it sends to the President might as well be called 'The Insurance Industry Profit Protection and Enhancement Act.'" Pelosi insisted that Congress had no intention of [failing to include a public option].*[10]

True to her word, Speaker Pelosi got the bill through the House of Representatives with the public option intact. But she had no control over the US Senate, where Joe Lieberman became the deciding vote, and he chose to kill the Medicare option, presumably at the behest of his funders.

As Lieberman told *Fox News*: "A public option plan is unnecessary. It has been put forward, I'm convinced, by people who really want the government to take over all of health insurance."[11]

And we definitely can't have that. After all, it may make us as efficient and effective at delivering healthcare as the rest of the developed world and save millions of lives over a few decades . . . but would cut off the hundreds of millions of dollars that health insurance industry executives take home every month. And, probably too, it would cut off their campaign contributions.

Wendell Potter: A Good Man in a Bad Job

Killing other people is probably the greatest taboo among humans, even when done indirectly or by proxy; it's why murder is the plot device for so many novels, TV shows, and movies. We're fascinated by things that are so grotesque, so far out of the everyday experience, so frightening, that most of us can barely imagine them in our own lives.

Yet far outside the realm of mobsters, warriors, and hit men, our nation harbors a small but very affluent class of people who take actions every day—proactive, knowing, intentional actions—that contribute to the deaths of their fellow Americans.

Wendell Potter was one of those people until he was so overwhelmed by his conscience that he resigned his solidly six-figure salary to take on the very corporations that had paid him to promote policies that led to other people's deaths.

In his 2010 book *Deadly Spin*, Potter tells the story of his awakening, the moment that pushed him over the edge from being a health insurance industry insider to a whistleblower.[12]

It was March 5, 2009, and President Obama was promoting what would become the Affordable Care Act. Potter, then the director of public relations at health insurance behemoth CIGNA, was "channel surfing for some news about [Obama's] healthcare reform summit . . . at the White House that day."

On MSNBC, host Tamron Hall was interviewing Zach Wamp, then Tennessee's Third District representative in the US House. "It's probably the next major step towards socialism," Wamp told Hall and the TV audience. "[T]his is literally a fast march towards socialism where the government is bigger than the private sector in our country, and healthcare's the next major step, so we ought all be worried about it."

Wamp then turned his rhetorical guns directly on low-income Americans and undocumented immigrants.

"The forty-five million people that (sic) don't have health insurance," he said, "about half of them choose not to have health insurance. . . . How many illegal immigrants are in this country today, getting our healthcare? Gobs of 'em!"

Potter felt his stomach drop. "As I listened to Wamp's rant," he wrote, "I knew exactly where he'd gotten his talking points: from me.

"He was using the same misleading, intentionally provocative, and xenophobic talking points that I had helped write."

Potter had served not only as the head of PR for CIGNA but also as a member of the Strategic Communications Advisory Committee for AHIP (America's Health Insurance Plans), the industry's largest trade and lobbying group; it was in that capacity that he'd written much of what had become Wamp's talking points.

That same night, AHIP's president, Karen Ignagni, also showed up on TV, telling President Obama how the insurance industry was on board with his effort.

"We want to work with you," she told Obama. "You have our commitment. We hear the American people about what's not working. We've taken that seriously." The industry had billions in profits at stake and, with Ignagni, was rolling out the biggest of the big guns.

"Ignagni," Potter wrote, "is one of the most effective communicators and—with a salary and bonuses of $1.94 million in 2008—one of the highest-paid special interest advocates in Washington. . . . She is smart, telegenic, articulate, charming, a strong leader, and a brilliant strategist. . . . Princeton economist Uwe Reinhardt commented, 'Whatever AHIP pays her is not enough.'"

Like Potter at that time, she was another of that small group of people who are more than willing to take money to promote policies that lead to the deaths of tens of thousands of Americans every year, according to Harvard University.[13] All to enhance corporate profits.

While watching Wamp use his talking points and seeing his AHIP boss, Ignagni, essentially lie to Obama marked the decision point for Potter, the process, for him, had begun a bit earlier, in December 2007, when his company, CIGNA, had refused to pay for a liver transplant for a Los Angeles teenager named Nataline Sarkisyan.

Her community had come together to protest CIGNA's decision, and the protests were picked up by a prominent local TV station, KTLA; from there the story went national.

Potter, as head of PR for CIGNA, took it on, although in this case it was so obvious that the insurance company's decision was a PR disaster that he argued within the company that they should just pay for Nataline's transplant and have done with it.

"For the first time, I started paying close personal attention to the case," Potter wrote in *Deadly Spin*. "As the father of a daughter just three years older than Nataline, I couldn't help putting myself in their shoes, wondering what life would be like for my wife and me if we were fighting with an insurance company to get it to cover a lifesaving transplant for our daughter, Emily. Just thinking about it caused me to ache."

Potter escalated the issue to his CIGNA boss, Carol Ann Petren, arguing that the company should just pay for the transplant and end the whole crisis.

Petren took it to CIGNA's CEO, Ed Hanway. They brought in CIGNA Healthcare's president, David Cordani, and the company's chief medical officer, Jeffrey Kang, MD.

All backed the company's decision to let Nataline die rather than pay for her transplant, so Potter's next step was to reach out to Kekst & Company, a PR firm that specialized in dealing with publicly traded companies in the midst of a PR crisis.

Nataline had now been waiting several days for the transplant, and a donor liver that would have been "perfect" had gone to another person because the hospital wouldn't operate as long as CIGNA refused to pay. Time was not on her side.

She was a Girl Scout and a popular student, and had dreams of becoming a fashion designer. Her parents were Armenian immigrants, and she spoke both English and Armenian fluently, so she volunteered with the Armenian Youth Federation to help kids with both languages.

As the story blew up in the media, the country learned that she prayed with her mother every night. "Just the two of us," her mother told the press. "We never missed a night."

To keep her spirits up during this ordeal with CIGNA, her father promised to buy her a white Ford Mustang when she graduated from high school.

Nataline's story by now had gone viral, with people across the country praying for her and organizing mass calls into CIGNA's various offices on her behalf.

Larry Rand, one of Kekst's founders, was blunt with CIGNA's senior executives. "Look, Carol, you have to make this go away," he told Petren in an emergency conference call. "Approve the transplant—now."

That call persuaded them to overrule their own policies and slightly dent corporate profits, just this one time, to save this particular teenager's life.

Writing that he was "relieved . . . for Nataline's family," Potter said he felt like a load had been lifted.

"I imagined how joyous and hopeful my wife and I would be," he wrote, "to hear from our insurance company—which would be CIGNA—that a procedure that might save [my daughter] Emily's life had been given 'clearance.'"

He tried to reach out to Nataline's family to let them know the good news, but they were at a protest put on by the California Nurses Association, headed by RoseAnn DeMoro. It took a few hours, but he finally got the good news to them, and the hospital began preparations for the surgery.

"But a few minutes after 10 p.m.," Potter wrote, "my phone rang at home. There would be no need for CIGNA to cover the transplant after all. Nataline had just died."

A few days later, Nataline was buried in a white coffin, a demand from her father, who was heartbroken that he'd never be able to give her the white Mustang he'd promised her.

The family hired "lawyer to the stars" Mark Geragos, who called for CIGNA to be prosecuted for murder or, at the least, manslaughter, as Nataline had been "maliciously killed" by the company and its executives' decisions. (Unfortunately, the industry long ago paid members of Congress enough that they wrote immunity from such lawsuits into federal laws that are so strong as to preempt state murder laws, as Potter documents in his book.)

"It finally dawned on me," Potter wrote, "that in my own quest for money and prestige, I had sold my soul."

He'd earlier seen an article in *Architectural Digest* about the 24-room mansion that CIGNA's former CEO, Wilson Taylor, had built in the hills of eastern Pennsylvania. There was even "a separate 'grandchildren's cottage'" with "stone columns imported from Europe." Taylor's salary had been $24 million in his last year, which didn't even include his stock options, traditionally the largest part of a CEO's compensation.

"When I read that article and saw the stunning pictures of Taylor's new place," Potter wrote, "it became clear to me, in ways that it hadn't before, that people enrolled in CIGNA's insurance plans had actually helped pay for that twenty-four-room stone manse with its seventeenth-century Spanish columns and its impossibly French kitchen."

It was paid for in large part with the money CIGNA kept by saying no to people needing medical care and then standing by as they deteriorated and died.

Potter's final job for CIGNA was announcing that, for the first three months of 2008, the company had brought in $4.6 billion in revenues and skimmed $265 million off the top as profit, in addition to other millions that went to the company's senior executives.

I've known Wendell Potter for over a decade now; he's a good and decent man who deeply regrets his role in what is arguably one of the most corrupt industries in the United States.

"I was a beneficiary of a lot of money that was paid to someone whose job doesn't even exist in most other countries," he told me on the radio some years ago.

Potter's current incarnation is starting, building, and running a news site with an emphasis on issues of health and labor; he named it Tarbell.org after Ida Tarbell, who pioneered investigative journalism (then called "muckraking") during the Gilded Age and wrote the definitive book on the most corrupt corporation of that era, John D. Rockefeller's Standard Oil.

With her help and exposé, the US government broke up Rockefeller's monopoly and returned some sanity to the oil business. Potter is today trying to do the same with healthcare.

"Dollar Bill" McGuire and the Privatization of Medicare

A billion dollars is a mind-bending amount of money. It's a million dollars a thousand times—more money than any human being could possibly need to live a full and satisfying life, and enough to ensure that children, grandchildren, and generations to come will never, ever have to work. It's dynastic money.

Yet that's what you can make in healthcare in America if you're willing to say to sick people, "No, I won't pay for that surgery or medication even though it may save your life."

"'Dollar Bill' has made lots of news with cash-and-stock paydays that have topped $100 million in recent years—and he's still sitting atop stock options valued at $1.6 billion," wrote Neal St. Anthony in 2007 for the *Minneapolis Star-Tribune*, the largest newspaper in UnitedHealth's home state of Minnesota.[14]

"Dollar Bill" was Bill McGuire, then the CEO of United-Health, the nation's largest health insurance operation. And although trained as a physician, McGuire didn't make his money healing anybody.

On the contrary, he made that money by aggressively enforcing the fine print in his company's contracts with people who'd bought health insurance from UnitedHealth, particularly that fine print that talked about preexisting conditions, lifetime caps, not paying "out-of-network expenses," and requiring doctors and hospitals to jump through a never-ending series of exhausting hoops to get "authorization" to treat sick people.

Not to mention his (and his senior executives') manipulation of stock options; after all, if you're going to run a grift on your customers, why not do the same to your shareholders?

The *Wall Street Journal* pointed out in March 2006 that McGuire had backdated some of his stock options, increasing his income by hundreds of millions in what the *Journal* called "one of the most lucrative stock-option grants ever."[15]

The Securities and Exchange Commission later agreed, and as Reuters reported the following year, McGuire had to "forfeit more than $400 million in stock options and other compensation and pay a $7 million fine to settle an investigation into the health insurer's options practices."[16]

In 2003, President George W. Bush and his congressional Republicans gave UnitedHealth a huge gift (which good-government advocates would argue was in exchange for massive lobbying and campaign contributions, so it was more of a quid pro quo). They carved a hole in Medicare, the government healthcare payment system for people over 65, and let private for-profit health insurance companies fill it.

This semi-privatization of Medicare was called Medicare Part C, or Medicare Advantage. Although it has the name "Medicare," it's not Medicare. It's private, for-profit insurance, with almost all of the costs paid for with funds extracted from the government's Medicare trust fund.

While Dollar Bill left UnitedHealth in 2006 with his billion-plus dollars (and a trail of dead and dying customers), the company jumped into Medicare Advantage with the same gusto for making money as it had under McGuire's stewardship.

The headline from Kaiser Health News, the gold standard publication for reporting on the healthcare industry in America, says it all: "UnitedHealth Doctored Medicare Records, Overbilled U.S. by $1 Billion, Feds Claim."[17]

In a massive fraud reminiscent of Republican Senator Rick Scott's 1990s tenure as CEO of Columbia/HCA, the hospital group that had to pay the government $1.7 billion for Scott's company's Medicare fraud,[18] UnitedHealth ripped off America in a way that could only be described as breathtaking. Or at least second only to Rick Scott.

"In a 79-page lawsuit filed in Los Angeles," Kaiser Health News reported, "the Justice Department alleged that the insurer made patients appear sicker than they were in order to collect higher Medicare payments than it deserved. The government said it had 'conservatively estimated' that the company 'knowingly and improperly avoided repaying Medicare' for more than a billion dollars over the course of the decade-long scheme."[19]

The "Advantage" War against Medicare

Medicare Advantage is a massive, trillion-dollar rip-off, of the federal government and of taxpayers, and of many of the people buying the so-called Advantage plans.

It's also one of the most effective ways that insurance companies could try to kill Medicare for All, since about a third of all people who think they're on Medicare are actually on these privatized plans instead.

Nearly from its beginning, Medicare has allowed private companies to offer plans that essentially compete with it, but they were an obscure corner of the market and didn't really take off until the Bush administration and Republicans in Congress rolled out the Medicare Modernization Act of 2003. This was the big chance for the GOP (and a few corporatist Democrats) to finally privatize Medicare, albeit one bite at a time.

That law created a brand known as Medicare Advantage under the Medicare Part C provision, and a year later it phased in what are known as *risk-adjusted* large-batch payments to insurance companies offering Advantage plans.

Medicare Advantage plans are not Medicare. They're private health insurance most often offered by the big for-profit insurance companies (although some nonprofits participate, particularly the larger HMOs), and the rules they must live by are considerably looser than those for Medicare.

Even more consequential, they don't get reimbursed directly on a person-by-person, procedure-by-procedure basis. Instead, every year, Advantage providers submit a summary to the federal government of the aggregate *risk score* of all their customers and, practically speaking, are paid in a massive lump sum.

The higher their risk score, the larger the payment. A plan with mostly very ill people in it will get much larger reimbursements than a plan with mostly healthy people. After all, the former will be costly to keep alive and healthy, while the latter won't cost much at all.

Profit-seeking insurance companies, being the predators that they are, have found a number of ways to raise their risk scores without raising their expenses. The classical strategies of tying people to in-network providers, denying procedures routinely during first-pass authorization attempts, and having very high out-of-pocket caps are carried over from regular health insurance systems to keep costs low and profits high.

But with Medicare Advantage, the big insurance companies have invented a whole new way to rip us all off while padding their bottom lines.

For example, many Medicare Advantage plans promote an annual home visit by a nurse or physician's assistant as a "benefit" of the plan. What the companies are doing, though, is trying to upcode their customers to make them seem sicker than they are to increase their overall Medicare reimbursement risk score.

"Heart failure," for example, can be a severe and expensive condition to treat . . . or a barely perceptible tic on an EKG that represents little or no threat to a person for years or even decades. Depression is similarly variable; if it lasts less than two weeks, there's no reimbursement; if it lasts longer than two weeks, it's called a "major depressive episode" and rapidly jacks up a risk score.

The home health visits are designed more to look for illnesses or *codings* that can increase risk scores than to find conditions that require medical intervention. They're so profitable that an entire industry of sending nurses out on behalf of the smaller insurance companies has sprung up.

In summer 2014, the Center for Public Integrity (CPI) published an in-depth investigative report titled *Why Medicare Advantage Costs Taxpayers Billions More Than It Should.*[20]

They found, among other things, that one of the most common scams companies were running involved that very scoring of their customers as being sicker than they actually were, so that their reimbursements were way above the cost of caring for those people.

Here are a few points from the report:

- "Risk scores of Medicare Advantage patients rose sharply in plans in at least 1,000 counties nationwide between 2007 and 2011, boosting taxpayer costs by more than $36 billion over estimated costs for caring for patients in standard Medicare."

- "In more than 200 of these counties, the cost of some Medicare Advantage plans was at least 25 percent higher than the cost of providing standard Medicare coverage."

- The report documents how risk scores rose twice as fast for people who joined a Medicare Advantage health plan as for those who didn't.

- Patients, the report lays out, never know how their health is rated because neither the health plan nor Medicare shares risk scores with them—and the process itself is so arcane and secretive that it remains unfathomable to many health professionals.

- "By 2009, government officials were estimating that just over 15 percent of total Medicare Advantage payments were inaccurate, about $12 billion that year."

- Based on its own sampling of data from health plans, the report shows how CMS has estimated that faulty risk scores triggered nearly $70 billion in what officials deemed "improper" payments to Medicare Advantage plans from 2008 through 2013.

- CMS decided, according to the report, not to chase after overcharges from 2008 through 2010 even though the agency estimated through sampling that it had made more than $32 billion in "improper" payments to Medicare Advantage plans over those three years. CMS did not explain its reasoning.

- The report documents how Medicare expected to pay the health plans more than $150 billion in 2014, the year the study was published.[21]

Companies are almost never nailed for these overcharges, and when they are, they usually pay back pennies on the dollar.

For example, when the Office of Inspector General, Health and Human Services (which oversees Medicare), audited six out of the hundreds of plans on the market in 2007, they found that just those six companies "had been overpaid by an estimated $650 million" for that one year. As the Center for Public Integrity states, "CMS settled five of the six audits for a total repayment of just over $1.3 million."[22]

The Centers for Medicare and Medicaid Services also, in 2012, decided to audit only 30 plans a year going forward. As CPI noted, "At that rate, it would take CMS more than 15 years to review the hundreds of Medicare Advantage contracts now in force." And that's 15 years to audit just one year's activity!

Things haven't improved since that 2014 investigative report from CPI. In September 2019, Senator Sherrod Brown of Ohio and five Democratic colleagues sent a letter to President Donald Trump's CMS administrator, Seema Verma.

"The recent HHS Payment Accuracy Report exposes that taxpayers have overpaid Medicare Advantage plans more than $30 billion . . . over the last three years," Brown wrote. "This report comes on the heels of a 2016 Government Accountability Office (GAO) report and a 2013 GAO report on [Medicare Advantage] plan overcharges and the failure of the Centers for Medicare and Medicaid (CMS) to recoup billions of dollars of improper payments from MA plans."[23]

Meanwhile, during the four years of the Trump administration, CMS went out of their way to *illegally* promote Medicare Advantage plans (which typically cost CMS far more than a regular Medicare plan).

A February 2020 report in the *New York Times* stated, "Under President Trump, some critics contend, the Centers for Medicare and Medicaid Services, which administers Medicare, has become a cheerleader for Advantage plans at the expense of original Medicare."[24]

The report pointed to the draft release of the 2019 *Medicare & You* handbook, which is mailed every year to all enrollees and posted online. "Advocates and some lawmakers criticized language describing Advantage as a less expensive alternative to original Medicare."

The National Bureau of Economic Research (NBER) compared Medicare Advantage with traditional Medicare and found the Advantage programs to be mind-bogglingly profitable: "MA insurer revenues are 30 percent higher than their healthcare spending. Healthcare spending for enrollees in MA is 25 percent lower than for enrollees in [traditional Medicare] in the same county and [with the same] risk score."

At the same time, Medicare Advantage often screws its customers. According to the NBER study, people with Medicare Advantage got 15 percent fewer colon cancer screening tests, 24 percent fewer diagnostic tests, and 38 percent fewer flu shots.[25]

Speculation is rife as to why CMS would allow—much less promote—privatized plans that cost Medicare far more than original Medicare to rip off taxpayers to the tune of billions of dollars a month.

One possibility is regulatory capture—people working in CMS know that if they go along and get along, very well-paid jobs are waiting for them at for-profit insurance companies after a few years of government service. This is a chronic problem at other regulatory agencies, particularly those overseeing pollution, pharmaceuticals, telecommunications, and banking.

Another answer is that the Bush administration—where Medicare Advantage started—was so enamored of the idea of privatizing Medicare to eventually destroy the program (George W. Bush campaigned extensively from the late 1970s through his presidency to privatize both Social Security and Medicare) that they turned a blind eye to abuses.

The Obama administration had other priorities, as they were trying to push through the Affordable Care Act and didn't want to upset the apple cart. And when Trump came into power, his folks saw anything that drained resources out of Medicare and into the pockets of multimillionaire health insurance executives—a group notoriously generous when it comes to making political contributions—as a plus.

You Are Locked-in to Medicare Advantage

A fellow I'd known decades ago recently bubbled back into conversation among a few of us who'd hung out together in New York back in the 1970s. Sam, I'll call him, had turned 65 and hadn't had employer-provided health insurance in years. He spent a few hours trying to figure out how to sign up for Medicare and then gave up, totally confused, decided he'd try again in a few months.

Unfortunately, his prostate intervened. When Sam started experiencing pain urinating, he visited a local "doc in a box" urgent care clinic, where they gave him a PSA test. The result was shocking: his PSA was so high that it was a virtual certainty he had prostate cancer, and possibly it had even metastasized, a situation that is the second-leading cause of cancer death in American men.[26]

Telling him that he'd be facing hefty doctor and hospital bills regardless of the outcome, the urgent care clinic signed him up for a Medicare Advantage plan offered by an affiliate that almost certainly paid them a commission for the sign-up. Sam was excited, though, because he now had insurance, and it was a "no dollar" plan that didn't cost him a penny.

Sam then got on the phone to find a urologist who specialized in cancer. He found that the best worked out of Memorial Sloan Kettering Cancer Center in New York, and, telling them he was "on Medicare," he made an appointment to see one of their top docs. A month later, when his appointment finally opened up, the person who was checking him into the system told him that he'd have to pay cash because his Advantage plan didn't include Sloan Kettering.

In fact, more than a third of *all* Medicare Advantage plans nationwide do *not* include *any* of the National Cancer Institute centers, and *none* of the Advantage plans offered in the New York City area include the nation's most famous one, Memorial Sloan Kettering Cancer Center.[27]

Shocked, Sam contacted Medicare to see if he could transfer from Medicare Advantage to regular Medicare. This all happened in fall 2020, so they told him that he could make the change during the "open enrollment period" of October 15 to December 7. He made the change and called Sloan Kettering back.

This time, they wanted to know what Medigap policy he'd signed up for to fill in the 20 percent of billing that Medicare doesn't cover. That sent Sam back to the internet and, ultimately, to an insurance agent, who told him that while Medigap plans can't refuse you because of preexisting conditions when you first sign up when you turn 65, if you shift from Medicare Advantage back to traditional Medicare after that first enrollment, particularly if you're older or sick, they can simply refuse to cover you.

Reporter Mark Miller wrote for the *New York Times* in February 2020 about Ed Stein, a 72-year-old man with bladder cancer and a Medicare Advantage plan that didn't cover the cancer docs in his area who specialized in his type of cancer. He tried to shift back to traditional Medicare to cover what promised to be complex and expensive surgery and chemotherapy. As Miller wrote, "That was when he ran up against one of the least understood implications of selecting Advantage when you enroll in Medicare: The decision is effectively irrevocable."[28]

At the end of 2020, my friend Sam still hadn't seen a doctor. This is the state of healthcare in America as it's been sliced and diced by the multibillion-dollar insurance industry.

Meanwhile, every fall, Americans are inundated with hundreds of millions of dollars' worth of TV, direct mail, and internet advertising for Medicare Advantage plans. And where does the money come from to pay for that advertising?

It comes from the same place that provided over $1 billion in personal income to the former CEO of UnitedHealthcare and funnels over $100 million a month in compensation to senior executives in the largest health insurance companies:

denying claims while collecting *risk adjustment* claims from your tax dollars and mine.

The simple solution to the Medicare Advantage problem is to kill off the program. It was just a Trojan horse to privatize Medicare, and its presence will make Medicare for All even harder to implement. At the same time, the 20 percent hole that the GOP insisted on for skin in the game with real Medicare needs to go, too.

A comprehensive Medicare for All program would eliminate both of these problems.

Rick Scott Killed Charlene Dill

When I was five and six years old, my dad had two jobs, selling Rexair vacuum cleaners and *World Book* encyclopedias door-to-door. We used to visit what my younger brothers and I called "the cheese store" every weekend in Lansing, Michigan, where we picked up powdered milk, giant blocks of processed American cheese, and a 20-pound bag of macaroni.

I still hate powdered milk and love mac and cheese.

Which is why Charlene Dill's story hit me so hard. In 2014, she was living pretty much the life my dad had—she was working several part-time jobs (housecleaning and babysitting) and had just added a gig selling vacuum cleaners. And, like my dad back then, she was just barely getting by while parenting three young children.

As her best friend, Kathleen Voss Woolrich, wrote at the time and later told me on the phone, "She paid her property taxes and took care of her little trailer, which she owned, and got all three of her kids to school and day care. She was a very responsible person."

My dad's heart condition didn't develop until he was in his 60s, and by then he'd been 40 years in a good union job and had excellent health insurance, even through his retirement. Charlene wasn't so lucky.

As Woolrich recounted, after feeling pain in her chest, Charlene "went to the emergency room in 2012 and was told she had heart issues and needed monitoring and medication. But the Florida Republican Party and Governor Rick Scott had turned down 51 billion federal dollars for [Obamacare's 2009] Medicaid expansion, so she had to work extra to pay for the meds, and the ER was her doctor's office."

On March 21, she was going to get together with Woolrich and her daughter, who'd essentially grown up with Charlene's kids, but first she had to earn a few more dollars to pay for her heart medication, which she'd been cutting back on because of its cost.

The Affordable Care Act would have paid for Charlene's doctor visits and medications, but the billionaire Koch brothers, in particular, were incensed by that prospect: they put up millions to fund advertising and PR campaigns, first to stop, and then to destroy, what Americans had started calling Obamacare.

Scott, who was heavily supported by the Koch brothers (they sent 40 paid staffers to Florida to help with his last gubernatorial campaign),[29] followed their libertarian line that taking money from rich people to pay for the healthcare of working poor people was a bad idea. After all, it might hurt their "incentive" to work a second or third job. Like Charlene Dill did.

When Obamacare was rolled out, the National Federation of Independent Business (NFIB) went on the attack, pressing a lawsuit that went all the way to the Supreme Court, *National Federation of Independent Business v. Sebelius.*

The NFIB likes to present itself as a representative of small business, but its CEO makes nearly $1 million a year, and, as Renée Feltz wrote for the *Guardian,*

> Past tax records reveal most of the NFIB's funding comes from Freedom Partners, whose nine-member board includes eight current or former key figures at Koch Industries and other Koch entities. More than 95% of the candidates it backs are Republican.
>
> While its representatives are often quoted in the media as proponents of small businesses, the group refuses to release its donor list and tends to lobby for policies that benefit billionaires and corporate interests.[30]

Nonetheless, the NFIB went into court as the protector of small businesses' rights, including the right to not have the government take money from the Koch brothers and their peers to pay for working people's healthcare.

Joined by 26 Republican-run states with politicians taking money from various Koch-funded enterprises and a few right-wing individuals, the NFIB claimed that requiring every state to expand Medicaid to cover their working poor was an unconstitutional form of coercion.

The Supreme Court agreed: states that didn't want their working poor people to have health insurance could opt out of the Obamacare Medicaid expansion.

Charlene Dill lost her chance to get her medications paid for, along with millions of Americans in other Republican-controlled states every year.[31]

In the early evening of March 21, 2014, after spending a day cleaning houses, she headed out to a lead in Kissimmee, a small town near her trailer in Orlando, where a family had indicated an interest in buying a Rainbow vacuum cleaner.

While she was in the middle of her sales pitch, her heart stopped, and she fell over, unconscious. The family she was visiting called an ambulance, and Charlene was taken to the Poinciana Medical Center, but she was already dead, at age 32.

"I am burying my best friend because of [Governor] Rick Scott and . . . the policies of the Republican Party . . . ," Kathleen Voss Woolrich wrote. "She is one of the 7 people who will die each day because the Florida House of Representatives Republicans and Tea Party decided that we are not worth living. We are not worth healthcare. We were not worth Medicaid expansion."[32]

Woolrich added, "I'll never have her back. I'll never see my friend again. I'll never have another day with her because of the [Florida] Republican House of Representatives."

Like most of his right-wing buddies, Scott had declined to expand Medicaid to low-income working people like Charlene. No rich person's money was going to pay for Florida's working people's healthcare!

(Ironically, Scott's hospital company, which he sold before becoming governor, paid a $1.7 billion fine[33] after being convicted of the largest Medicare fraud in the history of the country to that point, all on his watch.[34] He walked away with nearly $100 million, which he used to leverage himself into the governor's office and then the US Senate.)

Charlene's then-congressman, Alan Grayson, wrote for the *Tampa Bay Times*:

> One of my constituents, Charlene Dill, could not afford [health insurance]. . . . Charlene knew she had a heart problem, but she couldn't afford the medications and frequent visits to the doctor.
>
> She worked three jobs but earned only $11,000 last year. With only $11,000 to feed her three children, keep a roof over their heads and pay the property taxes on her trailer, Charlene couldn't afford standard health coverage. And because she made more than $5,400, she was not eligible for free or reduced-cost coverage under Florida Medicaid.

Grayson added, "This young mother didn't have to die."

And, indeed, she didn't have to die, and neither did thousands of other Floridians—a state where one in five people has no health insurance whatsoever.[35]

As Grayson wrote on April 19, 2014, "The federal government committed more than $50 billion to fund Florida's Medicaid expansion. You might think that our cash-strapped state would be clamoring for money to provide healthcare to the sick and poor. But you would be wrong. Republican ideologues in the Legislature refused the money. And now, Charlene Dill is gone."[36]

As Woolrich told me on the phone, "If I could have carried her body all the way up to Tallahassee and put it on the ground in front of these Republicans, I would have done it."

Charlene's heart condition was controllable with medication; all she needed was the money to pay for the drugs and the doctor visits. Money she was instead redirecting to her three young children, ages three, seven, and nine.

Children now without a mother.

Work to Live, or Live to Work?

The question is as old as the Enlightenment era of our early republic: Is the economy here to serve us, or are we here to serve those who control or own most of the economy?

This question was at the core of Adam Smith's 1759 book *The Theory of Moral Sentiments* and is touched on in his 1776 *The Wealth of Nations*. It's repeatedly echoed through our history.

In 1932, running for president, Franklin D. Roosevelt spoke at San Francisco's Commonwealth Club. He raised it there.

"The issue of government has always been," he said, "whether individual men and women will have to serve some system of government or economics, or whether a system of government and economics exists to serve the individual men and women."

Government, FDR believed, was the only force large and strong enough to bend the movers and shakers of the economy to the public benefit. The oligarchs of his day, he said, "have undertaken to be not businessmen, but princes," lording over the average people whom the economy is meant to serve.

Even worse, FDR said, after the Republican administrations of Harding, Coolidge, and Hoover produced the roaring twenties and the Republican Great Depression, Americans believed that those "princes" of business had seized the government of the United States itself and turned it against them.

"There came a growing feeling that government was conducted for the benefit of a few who thrived unduly at the expense of all," he said. At the very least, FDR said in that speech, invoking the ancient concept of noblesse oblige, politicians must be mindful of "the ethical conception that a ruler [bears] a responsibility for the welfare of his subjects."[37]

But what's included in that "welfare"?

The word is referenced twice in the Constitution, first in the Preamble (the Constitution is ratified to "promote the general Welfare"), and then in Article I, Section 8 ("The Congress shall have Power To lay and collect Taxes . . . to pay the Debts and provide for the common Defence and general Welfare of the United States").

The George Washington administration certainly believed this was adequate constitutional authority for the federal government to pay for healthcare; Congress passed and Washington implemented not only military hospitals but also a poorhouse in Washington, DC, that provided food, clothing, shelter, and medical care.

Washington was followed in 1797 by President John Adams, who, on July 6, 1798, signed the Act for the Relief of Sick and Disabled Seamen, leading to the opening of a government-funded hospital on Castle Island in Boston Harbor in 1799. In addition to its government subsidy, the plan deducted 20 cents a month from the seamen's wages; its first chief physician was Dr. Thomas Welsh, who'd also fought during the Revolutionary War both in the Battle of Bunker Hill and at Lexington.[38]

The hospital was not for the Navy, though—because trans-oceanic transportation was so vital to the new American economy, this was for men who worked on civilian commercial ships, merchant seamen.

So it couldn't be argued that America had never considered providing government-funded healthcare to its citizens; indeed, we've been doing it since the founding of our republic.

But even the great FDR—with all his political and rhetorical skills—was unable to get healthcare to all Americans.

He and his secretary of labor, Frances Perkins (arguably the author of most of the New Deal), had pushed to include health insurance in the legislation that would become, in 1935, what we call Social Security, but it was a long shot.

Edwin E. Witte was the chairman of FDR's Committee on Economic Security (CES), tasked with determining what would and wouldn't be in the Social Security program that the new administration was putting together after big Democratic congressional gains in the 1934 election.

In a passing side note to his report to FDR, Witte told a 1955 audience on the 20th anniversary of Social Security, he had "merely stated that the CES would make a later report on the subject . . . with a provision that the Social Security Board should study the need for and possibility of improving the social security protection of Americans, including, among others, health insurance."

When Republicans read that reference to the need for "study" of the "possibility" of, among other things, "health insurance," it was as if a bomb had gone off in the Capitol.

"This innocent reference to health insurance," Witte told his audience, "led to the first special Meeting of the House of Delegates of the American Medical Association, in the false belief that the Administration was secretly trying to foist compulsory health insurance on the country. Immediately, the members of the Ways and Means Committee, then considering the social security bill in executive sessions, were deluged with telegrams from all parts of the country protesting against this 'nefarious plot.'"[39]

FDR decided that even *thinking* or *talking* about a national health insurance program could sink Social Security, so, according to Witte, he decided to put it off for the moment. FDR again promised to work on a national health insurance program in his 1945 State of the Union address. "An expanded social security program," he told Congress, "and adequate health and education programs, must play essential roles in a program designed to support individual productivity and mass purchasing power."[40]

Three months later he was dead.

But that September, President Harry Truman picked up the issue, calling for a "Fair Deal" that included "extending, expanding and improving our entire social security program."[41] Truman, ever the blunt, plainspoken "man from Missouri," appealed to America's conscience.

"I put it to you, is it un-American to visit the sick, aid the afflicted, or comfort the dying? I thought that was simple Christianity."

PART TWO

The Origins of America's Sickness-for-Profit System

Germany Gets the World's First
Single-Payer System in 1884

The first modern workers' national single-payer Medicare for All–type health insurance program started in Germany in the late 1800s.

And while we frequently hear about "Bismarck's workers' insurance," Chancellor Otto von Bismarck ("The Iron Chancellor") didn't develop the program out of some enlightened sense of human dignity or workers' rights. Workers in the streets pushed him to it.

Karl Marx was a German economist and philosopher who argued that two pillars held up modern capitalism: the bourgeois business and factory *owner* class and the proletariat *worker* class, which made production of things possible through their labor.

Much of his theory had to do with the inherent conflict between these two classes and how workers might overcome oppression by capitalists by banding together into unions or cooperatives, or by creating new forms of government that prioritized labor over capital.

When he published *The Communist Manifesto* in 1848 and *Das Kapital* (*Capital*) in 1867, his work created a political explosion all over the world, leading to armed revolutions in Russia and China (among others) in the early and mid-20th century.

But Marx was widely read immediately upon publication in Germany in particular, where his following was so broad and strong that it inspired the 1863 creation of the Sozialdemokratische Partei Deutschlands, or Social Democratic Party of Germany (SDP), today the second-largest political party in that nation.[1]

The German Empire was formed in 1871, after Bismarck defeated France in the Franco-Prussian War, and lasted until the formation of the German constitutional Weimar Republic in 1919, following Germany's defeat in World War I. Almost immediately after the Empire's formation, followers of Marx rose up across the nation arguing for worker protections and limits on capitalism.[2]

Bismarck, who ruled as German chancellor from 1871 to 1890, was alarmed by Marxism and the SDP and, from 1878 until he left office, banned the SDP from meeting altogether. That didn't stop the party or its members from their activism, though, and by the early 1880s the SDP had become a major force in German politics through a variety of proxies.

This coincided with the explosion of the industrial revolution, which seized Germany more than the rest of Europe: the country was rapidly industrializing, and workers' strikes and other labor actions were often put down by both private goons hired by employers and the police.

Fearing a backlash from workers now set afire with Marx's ideas, Bismarck decided that a small, reasonable amount of socialism—a national healthcare and workers' compensation system for working people—would calm the worker complaints while actually making German industry more competitive. (Both turned out to be true.)

He first introduced his single-payer proposal in 1881, but conservatives in the government fought bitterly against it. They called him a socialist and accused him of attacking "freedom."

In a moment reminiscent of the GOP's epic and recurrent assertion that Obamacare would abolish the American "right" to die uninsured in the street outside a hospital,[3] Bismarck took the argument head-on.

"If one argues against my position that this is socialism," he said in an 1884 speech to the German Parliament, "then I do not fear at all. The question is, where do the justifiable limits of state socialism lie?"[4]

It was a question that the entire nation was then debating, and workers were daily in the streets demanding both better pay and a national workers' compensation system that would protect them when hurt in those early, dangerous factories.

"Each law for poor relief is socialism," Bismarck said. "There are states that distance themselves so far from socialism that poor laws do not exist at all. I remind you of France."

At the time, France was spending a fortune in the Sino-French War, seizing large parts of Vietnam and moving toward the Chinese border. The French Third Republic was dominated by conservatives and the Catholic Church, both steadfastly opposed to anybody but the Church providing any sort of welfare or other support to working or poor people.

Tuberculosis was also ravaging France at the time, leading to a national call for a public health program, at the very least, but conservatives fought it so successfully that the debate was essentially postponed a full generation until 1902.[5]

Referring to one of the principal opponents of a German national healthcare and workers' compensation system, Bismarck said, "This man expresses the French view that every

French citizen has the right to starve and that the state has no responsibility to hinder him in the exercise of this right."

Bismarck put the argument squarely into the realm of national defense and state security. Without a national system to protect German workers, he said, the working class and the "oppressed and suffering among us" would continue to threaten political stability.

"In my opinion," he said, "a primary reason for the success that the leaders of the real Social Democracy have had . . . lies in the fact that the state does not promote enough state social-ism; it allows a vacuum to form in a place where it should be active, and this is filled by others, by agitators who poke their nose into the state's business."

Returning to the argument that "freedom" means a lack of support by the state, he called out the skeptics in his own conservative party. "Gentlemen," he said, "freedom is a vague concept; no one has a use for the freedom to starve."

American conservatives have argued for years that because tax laws are enforced by the power of the state—which includes the power to use guns and jails to enforce the law—taxation is a form of "violence."

It was a popular argument in Bismarck's time as well, as members of his own conservative party argued against expanding taxation to pay for his healthcare program. One spoke up to say that Germans would be "forced" to pay for the system, and this was anti-freedom.

"The expression, 'If you aren't willing, I'll use force' is totally unjustified," Bismarck said. "There scarcely exists nowadays a word with which more abuse is committed than the word *free*."

Calling out his detractors, he said, "According to my experience, everyone understands by *freedom* [these conservatives mean] only the freedom for oneself and not for others. . . . In short, by *freedom* they actually mean *domination*."

And this was the real crux of the issue, Bismarck said, stating that "the freedom of the princes from the emperor, and the power of the nobles over the serfs . . . that means, *to be free* was for them identical with the concept *to dominate*. They do not feel themselves free unless they dominated [working people].

"Therefore, whenever I read the word *free* before another adjective, I become very suspicious."

Deputy Ludwig Bamberger, Bismarck's most prominent critic, spoke out to call the idea of a national single-payer health insurance program a "socialist fad." Bismarck was furious. "Perhaps the whole institution of the state is a socialist fad," he replied. "If everyone could live on his own, perhaps everyone would be much more free, but also much less protected and guarded."

Summarizing his challenge to Bamberger, he said, "If the Deputy calls the proposal a socialist whim, I reply simply that it is untrue." Instead, he said, a national health insurance program would strengthen both the workers and the state itself.

"Do not doubt," Bismarck said in his speech's last sentence, "that we are acting honorably to strengthen the domestic peace, and particularly the peace between worker and employer . . . without exposing the commonwealth to new dangers."

Bismarck got his national healthcare system, his workers' compensation system, and even a Social Security–like system of old-age pensions in 1883, 1884, and 1889, respectively, and shortly thereafter Austria and Hungary did the same.[6] It set the stage for the rest of Europe and, later, industrializing Japan, Taiwan, and South Korea to do the same.

Today, over a century later, the only developed nation in the world with a dominant political party that considers a lack of these things to represent "freedom"? The United States of America.

America, the Land of the Sick

America is the only developed country in the world that doesn't recognize healthcare as a human right, the only country with more than two-thirds of its population lacking access to affordable healthcare, and the only country in the developed world that has, since its founding, continuously enslaved and legally oppressed and disenfranchised a large minority of its population because of their race.

Prior to the Trump Depression, roughly 60 percent of Americans would have had to take out a loan or otherwise borrow or beg for money to deal with a single, unexpected $1,000 expense;[7] the number now is probably closer to 80 percent of Americans who can't handle such a hit and is higher still for minority communities.

Yet copays and deductibles when a person gets sick *averaged* $1,318 in 2015, when the Kaiser Family Foundation did a comprehensive survey of Americans, up from $548 just 10 years earlier.[8] This strikes minorities particularly hard, which, it turns out, is not an accident.

The simple fact is that, were it not for slavery, white supremacy, and the legacy of "scientific racism," America would have had a national, single-payer healthcare system in 1915, just

31 years after Germany put into place the modern world's first such program.

At the center of the effort to prevent a national healthcare system—or any form of government assistance that may even incidentally offer benefit to African Americans—were Frederick Ludwig Hoffman and the Prudential Life Insurance Company, which promoted his "science based" racial theories to successfully fight single-payer health insurance.

Frederick Ludwig Hoffman
Makes a Discovery

Racism is the main reason that America doesn't consider healthcare a human right and provide it to all citizens, as does every other developed country in the world. Racist whites, particularly in the South, have worked for over a century to make sure that healthcare is hard for Black people and other minorities to get.

And their biggest ally, their founding spokesperson in the post–Civil War era, their biggest champion right up to the 1940s, was a man that most Americans have never heard of.

In 1884, 19-year-old Frederick Ludwig Hoffmann left Germany for America after failing at a number of job attempts and being rejected for the German Army because he was "physically deficient" and frail, standing five-foot-seven and weighing a mere 110 pounds. He arrived in New York with $4.76 in his pocket, speaking "not a word of English" but determined to prove wrong his mother's assessment that he was a "good-for-nothing."[9]

From this humble beginning, Hoffman went on to become one of America's most influential statisticians and analysts of public health, making numerous consequential discoveries about how industrialization was killing American workers.

He dropped the last *n* in his last name, became so fluent in English that his accent was nearly indistinguishable, and married into an upscale Georgia family. By 1920, he was an American citizen, vice president of America's largest insurance company, and a national authority on the now-discredited pseudoscience called *scientific racism*.

In 1908, his article "The Mortality from Consumption [tuberculosis] in the Dusty Trades," published by the US Department of Labor, produced the first national efforts to reduce lung damage in the workplace. He also published the first work (1915) linking tobacco to lung cancer.

From this, he became vice president of the National Tuberculosis Association (today known as the American Lung Association) and later demonstrated the connection between exposure to asbestos and the disease that killed my father, mesothelioma (a bit of data that asbestos companies worked to keep hidden for the next 80 years).

In 1913, Hoffman wrote a seminal paper on the relationship between workplace pollution and cancer, which led him to cofound the American Society for the Control of Cancer (known today as the American Cancer Society). In 1937, he extended his research beyond the workplace and published *Cancer and Diet: With Facts and Observations on Related Subjects*, a book correctly pointing out the correlation between poor nutrition and cancer that is still in print at a dense 767 pages, mostly of statistical analysis between dietary habits and rates of disease.

His cancer research was so extensive and detailed (he concluded that diets heavy in processed foods and animal products produced higher cancer rates) that Adelle Davis—whose books were my mother's nutrition guru in the 1950s and '60s—became an early "convert" and "a devotee of Frederick Hoffman."[10]

But Hoffman's most controversial lifelong obsession was with the relationship between disease, race, and society.

On one of his first trips to Georgia, he wrote, he came across a book by Dr. Eugene R. Corson, a Georgia obstetrician, titled *The Vital Equation of the Colored Race and Its Future in the United States*.[11] It was apparently an updated or shortened version of Corson's widely read "The Future of the Colored Race in the United States From an Ethnic and Medical Standpoint," published in 1887 in the *New York Medical Times*.[12]

This was just after the failure of Reconstruction, and a widespread topic of speculation, particularly in the South, was whether Black people would soon outnumber white people in that part of the country. The Ku Klux Klan and others calling for wholesale slaughter and suppression of Black people claimed that they were more likely to have larger families because they were "more prolific," code for "excessively sexual," a charge that had persisted from the earliest days of slavery and led to the murder of Emmett Till (among others).

However, the "scientific" racists of the day, like Corson, thought differently. Corson led a movement suggesting that people of African ancestry, now lacking the protective womb of slavery, would die out for the simple reason that the Black race was inferior to whites.

Corson acknowledged the Klan's argument that "the simpler the organism, the simpler the genesis and the greater the prolificness." But, he said, white people would prevail because they were less likely to die of disease, citing Herbert Spencer's "Theory of Population Deduced from the General Law of Animal Fertility."[13]

While Black people might have more children, Corson wrote, white people would still outnumber them because Black fecundity "is more than compensated for by the ability [of white people] to maintain individual life."

Enslaved people from Africa had found themselves in a civilization "of which [they are] not a product" and thus were less likely to be successful in "the struggle for existence." Therefore, Corson wrote, Black people "must suffer physically, a result which forbids any undue increase in the race."

The discovery of this theory, called the *racial extinction thesis*, electrified Hoffman, and he spent the rest of his life promoting it, while campaigning to stop any sort of movement toward a national health insurance program that might prevent or slow down the extinction of Black people in America.

Race Traits and Tendencies of the American Negro

In August 1896, the American Economic Association published a book that represented a turning point in Frederick Hoffman's life and sealed the fate of single-payer health insurance in America. It was Hoffman's magnum opus, summarizing decades of compiled statistics on Black versus white mortality, proving, according to Hoffman, once and for all, that for Black people, "gradual extinction is only a question of time."[14]

In *Race Traits and Tendencies of the American Negro*, Hoffman set out not only to repeatedly make and statistically prove the above claim, but also to prove that anytime white people tried to help Black people, particularly by offering them healthcare services, the result was disaster for both.

Noting that "the Negro has failed to gain a foothold in any of the northern states," Hoffman wrote, "he is in the South as a permanent factor . . . with a tendency to drift into the cities, there to concentrate in the most undesirable and unsanitary sections . . . and the evil effect will be more felt by the cities which are thus augmented in population of an undesirable character."[15]

In great detail, Hoffman spent about 300 pages documenting, with exhaustive tables and statistics, the fact that Black people were more likely to die as a result of everything from malaria to tuberculosis to childbirth.

And it was all because of their race.

"The decrease in the rate of increase of the colored population has been traced first to the excessive mortality, which in turn has been traced to an inferior vital capacity. . . . This racial inferiority has, in turn, brought about a moral deterioration . . . sexual immorality . . . diminished social and economic efficiency . . ."

And that represented a danger to white people, Hoffman wrote.

The participation of freed Black people in the contemporary labor pool and in society overall, he wrote, "in the course of years must prove not only a most destructive factor in the progress of the colored race, but also in the progress, social as well as economic, of the white race brought under its influence."

Slavery had actually been good for Black people, Hoffman believed, and the abolition of slavery at the end of the Civil War was only going to speed up the demise of that race.

"Nothing is more clearly shown from this investigation," he wrote, "than that the southern black man at the time of emancipation was healthy in body and cheerful in mind. He neither suffered inordinately from disease nor from impaired bodily vigor."

But with abolition, former slaves were "tending toward a condition in which matters will be worse than they are now, when diseases will be more destructive, vital resistance still lower, when the number of births will fall below the deaths, and gradual extinction of the race will take place."

While Hoffman pioneered linking causal conditions such as asbestos and carcinogen exposure to sickness, he was so blinded by racism that a modern reader of his book constantly finds himself shouting, "But these things are also true of poor whites! These are caused by discrimination and poverty!!"

At the time, though, the vast majority of white Americans agreed with him. He was echoing the white cultural and scientific consensus of the late 19th and early 20th centuries when he wrote, "Given the same conditions of life for two races, the one of Aryan descent will prove the superior, solely on account of its ancient inheritance of virtue and transmitted qualities which are determining factors in the struggle for race supremacy. The lower races, even under the same conditions of life, must necessarily fail because the vast number of incapables which a hard struggle for life has eliminated from the ranks of the white races, are still forming the large body of the lower races."

And, according to Hoffman and the other white "scientific racists," the problem wasn't just physical inferiority. The deepest "problem of the Negro," Hoffman wrote, was moral: "All the facts prove that a low standard of sexual morality is the main and underlying cause of the low and anti-social condition of the race at the present time. . . . The conclusion is warranted that it is merely a question of time when the actual downward course, that is, a decrease in the population will take place. In the meantime, however, the presence of the colored population is a serious hindrance to the economic progress of the white race."

For those well-intentioned white people who wanted to help out the people who were a mere generation or two away from slavery, Hoffman (and his colleagues, including the Prudential Life Insurance Company) had one simple bit of advice: *Don't even try.*

From Scientific Racism to Libertarianism

In 1980, David Koch famously ran for vice president of the United States under the banner of the Libertarian Party, an organization founded a few decades earlier by big business to give an economic rationale and political patina to their simple theory that economics were more important than democracy, and the quality of life of working people should be decided in the "free marketplace" instead of by unions or through democratic processes via government regulation.

In this, Koch and his Libertarian friends were echoing Frederick Hoffman.

In his 1896 book *Race Traits*, Hoffman laid out his "scientific" assertion that when government steps in to help people, it invariably ends up hurting them instead. Not only should there be no government assistance given to help African Americans recover from three centuries of property theft, forced labor, and legal violence, but it is scientifically wrong to even consider the idea.

White people and government programs to better the lives of Black people, Hoffman wrote, deserve "the most severe condemnation of modern attempts of superior races to lift inferior races to their own elevated position." The damage done to Black people by offering them any sort of help, government assistance, or even a minimum wage, he wrote, is "criminal" behavior for a "civilized people."

Hoffman pointed to Native Americans to prove his point. "Few races have made such a brave struggle for their own preservation; few races can boast of so high a degree of aboriginal civilization. . . . An iron will can be traced upon the countenance of nearly every Indian of note."

But it was government help, Hoffman wrote, that destroyed the American Indian.

It wasn't "adulterated whiskey nor the frightful consequences of sexual immorality, spread around the forts and settlements of the whites," that was "sufficient" to destroy Native Americans. It was charity.

"The most subtle agency of all," he wrote, sounding like Ronald Reagan or David Koch, "governmental pauperism, the highest development of the theory of easy conditions of life, did what neither drink nor the poisons of venereal disease could do, and today the large majority of the tribes are following the Maories and Hawaiians towards the goal of final extinction."

White Americans rationalized their brutality toward Native Americans and African Americans by saying that it was simple evolutionary biology: only the strong survive, and when the weak are allowed to propagate, it weakens the overall human race.

"Easy conditions of life and a liberal charity are among the most destructive influences affecting the lower races," Hoffman concluded, "since by such methods the weak and incapable are permitted to increase and multiply, while the struggle of the more able is increased in severity [by the increase in taxes and regulation]."

And it's not just charity. "All the facts prove," Hoffman wrote, "that education, philanthropy, and religion have failed to develop [among Black people] a higher appreciation of the stern and uncompromising virtues of the Aryan race.

"Instead of making the race more independent, modern educational and philanthropic efforts have succeeded in making it even more dependent on the white race at the present time than it was previous to emancipation."

Free education—as any Libertarian can tell you—is more dangerous to the souls of people than slavery. And free healthcare is even worse.

Sounding like a modern-day acolyte of Ayn Rand, Hoffman wrote, "Instead of clamoring for aid and assistance from the white race, the negro himself should sternly refuse every offer of direct interference in his own evolution. The more difficult his upward struggle, the more enduring will be the qualities developed."

And, like Ayn Rand, David Koch, and Ronald Reagan, Hoffman believed that these were eternal truths independent of race.

"No missionary or educator or philanthropist extended aid or comfort to the English peasant class during its darkest days, to the earliest settlers on the coast of New England, or the pioneer in the forests of the far West. . . . [I]t is extremely rare to find a case where easy conditions of life or liberal charity have assisted man in his upward struggle. Self reliance . . . must be developed, and thus far have not been developed by the aid of charity or liberal philanthropy."

This libertarian ideal is still pervasive in our modern fragmented healthcare system, and in the midst of the COVID-19 crisis in 2020, it resulted in thousands of daily American deaths, disproportionately hitting racial minorities.

New York Shakes Up the Insurance Industry

Blame the plutocrats' costume balls for the crisis in the insurance industry at the turn of the century, a crisis that led to blocking a national single-payer health insurance system.

In 1905, the Legislature of the state of New York was provoked by a public outcry to investigate the life insurance business. The New York lawmakers authorized an investigative body led by State Senator William Armstrong, later known as the Armstrong Commission, which held 51 investigatory sessions leading to eight new laws to regulate the industry.

The event not only cemented the reputation of Armstrong but also kicked off the political career of Charles Evans Hughes, propelling him to the governorship of New York, the Republican presidential nomination in 1916, and the chief justiceship of the US Supreme Court in 1930.

And it was a costume ball that triggered much of the public outrage.

Eight years earlier, in February 1897, New York billionaire (in today's money) banker and attorney Bradley Martin and his wife, Cornelia, had thrown a costume ball at the Waldorf. They'd taken over the entire hotel, booking every single room, as the *New York Times* reported, and "all outside windows [were] boarded up" to keep the riffraff from seeing in.[16]

Mrs. Martin came dressed as Mary Stuart (wearing a necklace once owned by the queen), her husband as the Sun King, Louis XIV. John Jacob Astor, who would die on the *Titanic* in 1912, was dressed as Henry of Navarre, while J. P. Morgan was Molière.

Instead of a success, though, the party became a scandal; there was such ostentatious wealth on display that New York clergymen, progressive politicians, and many of the city's newspapers condemned the Martins.

"Some crank" sent a bomb to the Martins' home, according to the *Times*, because of all the controversy. New York's police commissioner told the *Times*, "The sensational articles that have recently appeared in two of the papers have started up these cranks to talking and writing against the Bradley Martins, and undoubtedly Mrs. Martin has been subjected to a great deal of annoyance from them."[17]

The Martins were so offended, humiliated, and frightened by the response of the good citizens of New York that they bought the former home of "Diamond King" Barney Barnato, what the *Times* said was "the most pretentious [home] in London," and moved to England.

Like the roaring twenties and today's late Reaganomics era, the Gilded Age was marked by obscene wealth and excess, contrasted with low wages and poverty for working people. Thus, when it was reported that James Hazen Hyde, son of the founder of the Equitable Life Assurance Society and a billionaire in today's money, had not only held a Versailles-themed ball himself but put it on the tab of the company, New York exploded. The Armstrong Commission investigation was the result of the tipping point that these two events hit, and it reflected so badly on Hyde that, like Martin, he fled the country, going to live in France.

The Armstrong Commission also found widespread evidence of bribery, or at least inappropriate influence, of politicians by insurance industry executives and recommended laws barring any employee of that industry from giving money to any politician, a harbinger of the Tillman Act of 1907, which banned corporate money contributions to federal candidates.

The scandals uncovered by Armstrong also fed a growing movement to provide every New Yorker with health insurance provided by nonprofit mutual companies and paid for by the state and the employers.

And Frederick Hoffman would help put a stop to it.

From Scientific Racism to "No Compulsory Healthcare!"

The "compulsory health insurance" (what today we'd call Medicare for All) movement of the early 20th century was as much (and possibly more) about getting paid sick leave as it was about covering doctor visits and hospitalization, because healthcare was so cheap that an unpaid week at work was a bigger hit to the wallet.

But workers wanted both.

The most successful effort of the era came out of an organization that a small group of progressive economists put together in 1905 and 1906, known as the American Association for Labor Legislation (AALL).

Their initial efforts were directed at paid sick leave, workers' compensation insurance, child labor laws, and workplace safety standards. To that last end, they were actively using the kinds of statistical analysis that Frederick Hoffman had both used and popularized to do everything from laying out his theories on race to showing an association between tobacco use and lung cancer.

Hoffman joined the AALL to promote their efforts.

A charitable reading of his motivations was that his statistical research on workplace phosphorus poisoning and lung disease overlapped with their efforts, and they were an organization that, at that time, was held in high regard. He did, after all, consider himself—and was, in a very real way—a major force for reform in public health and workplace safety arenas.

A less charitable motivation is posited in Daniel T. Rodgers's 1998 book *Atlantic Crossings: Social Politics in a Progressive*

Age.[18] Rodgers wrote, "On the AALL social insurance committee, he became the [Prudential] company's mole. . . . Hoffman took credit for blocking the drafting of any resolutions at the AALL's social insurance conference in 1913. During the framing of the association's model health insurance bill, he dragged his feet, obstructed, pressed in vain for company initiatives in the medical insurance field, and informed his employers—more and more certain that public health insurance was 'distinctly pernicious and a menace to our interests.'"

Despite Prudential and Hoffman's efforts, government-funded health insurance was gaining popularity in America (and being considered or adopted in Europe).

In 1912, Theodore Roosevelt made a third-party bid for the presidency, forming the Progressive Party (with its Bull Moose logo), and called for "the protection of home life against the hazards of sickness, irregular employment and old age through the adoption of a system of social insurance." Jane Addams (Hull House founder), dressed in suffragette white, seconded Roosevelt's nomination to wild cheers and applause; Roosevelt rallies routinely drew tens of thousands of people, and more than 200,000 people showed up in Los Angeles to support him and the party.[19]

Roosevelt's endorsement of "social insurance," including health coverage, both reflected and reinforced a growing national sentiment, and in 1915 the AALL called for every state to support a program of health insurance. Prudential hadn't yet gotten into the business of insuring health (they would in 1925), but they could see the writing on the wall.

What finally blew up Hoffman's support of the AALL apparently had to do with a system of insurance that had started in the late 17th century in the United Kingdom to cover fire losses and had gradually grown to include other forms of protection.

It was called *mutual insurance* and was distinct from Prudential's model in that the companies were owned by their policyholders instead of traditional corporate stockholders.

In this regard, mutual insurance companies ran much like employee-owned co-ops and lived in the nonprofit world both practically and philosophically. They also had lower operating costs, as they didn't have to shovel wheelbarrows of cash to their stockholders and senior executives.

America had a tradition of mutual insurance that started in 1752 with a company known as "the Philadelphia Contributionship for the Insurance of Houses From Loss by Fire." Its founder was Benjamin Franklin and it still exists; the idea of mutual property and casualty insurance companies grew from there across the states and around the world.[20]

In 1916, the AALL endorsed health insurance provided through a network of local and statewide mutual companies and called for those policies to also provide a small death benefit to cover funeral costs, which would have competed directly with the funeral coverage that was Prudential's main cash cow.

Hoffman wrote to the company, "We, of course, cannot compete with Compulsory Insurance, including a death benefit of, say $100."[21] He then resigned "in disgust" from the AALL and begin a campaign, sponsored by Prudential, to stop nonprofit, state-funded health insurance.

Hoffman and Prudential weren't alone in their concern: the Insurance Federation of New York told their members, "This is only the entering wedge; if once a foothold is obtained it will mean attempts to have such State Insurance of all kinds including fire."[22]

The AALL produced model legislation that was taken up in 1916 by eight states, including California and New York, the former via a ballot initiative and the latter in the New York legislature. In addition to calling for policies that would pay all costs of healthcare, the AALL's legislation called for up to 26 weeks of paid sick leave.

Picking up steam, the American Medical Association endorsed the AALL's model legislation as well. The battle was joined.

Prudential Helps Kill America's First Healthcare-for-All Campaign

Hoffman's Prudential-sponsored campaign to prevent any state from adopting a statewide nonprofit health (and death benefit) insurance program went into overdrive through 1916–1920. He traveled to Germany several times to chronicle, in minute detail, the failings of the kaiser's system that had been operating since 1885.

Prudential, in 1905, had been swept up in New York's Armstrong Investigation, and so, as historian Beatrix Hoffman (no relation to Frederick) wrote, "[b]ecause of their industry's public image problems, insurance executives knew their opposition to compulsory health insurance would be perceived as brazen self-interest."[23]

They needed a front man, and the guy who was famous for discovering the causes of numerous public health crises was perfect. Thus, Frederick Hoffman became the most well-known face of a massive, multiyear effort to stop the AALL's campaign. He was remarkably effective.

In the years between 1916, when he resigned from AALL, and 1920, when nonprofit state-funded health insurance finally died, Hoffman wrote numerous pamphlets trashing the German single-payer government health system, "exposing" corruption in the British efforts at a National Health Service, and arguing that America's healthcare system would be thrown into chaos and crisis if the AALL's programs were adopted.

His work was widely distributed, as historian Daniel Rodgers noted: "The Prudential saturated the state capitols with his pamphlets."[24]

His 1917 pamphlet *Facts and Fallacies of Compulsory Health Insurance*, and the subsequent *More Facts and Fallacies of Compulsory Health Insurance*, published two years later, were his most widely cited and most consequential writings. Historian Beatrix Hoffman wrote that the *Facts* pamphlet "resembled *Race Traits and Tendencies* in its impressive presentation of statistics and graphs alongside passionate polemics." Frederick Hoffman refuted every figure the Progressives used in defense of their plan, from "Misleading Data on German Longevity" to "Misleading Estimate of Cost" and "Disregard of Actuarial Methods."[25]

Appealing to the Daniel Boone mythos of rugged, independent individualism that didn't require assistance from government, Frederick Hoffman wrote in *More Facts and Fallacies of Compulsory Health Insurance*, "The ever-present menace to democracy and liberty is the perversion of the legislative function [toward providing health insurance]."[26]

Lawmakers and the public, Hoffman wrote as America was fighting Germany during World War I, were supporting state-funded health insurance, "which is unnecessary, and as essentially a product 'made in Germany' as any legislative panacea brought forward for the alleged good of the people during a generation or more. The propaganda had its origin in the program laid down by the International Association for Labour Legislation, which held its first meeting in Basel, Switzerland."[27]

Hoffman went on to say, "The proposed legislation strikes one more blow at self-dependence and initiative and makes your citizen a subject, whether of king or of commission matters little. Self-dependence and initiative, virtues only permitted to a few favored individuals in older forms of government, are again to be taken away from a large number of citizens, in return for a mess of pottage, and the normal cycle of human stupidity becomes obvious. The Constitution promised liberty and happiness, not supervision and comfort; that is, the guarantees were moral, not material."

Citing a 1917 report from the New Jersey Commission on Old Age, Insurance and Pensions, Hoffman wrote, "Under any and every system of social insurance the development of autocratic and arbitrary methods of interference with personal rights and liberties is a foregone conclusion."

Quoting the Bureau of Labor Statistics, Hoffman wrote, "[T]he State should concentrate its efforts on preventive work rather than on the attempt to cure diseases through insurance; in that the Workmen's Compensation Act had already taken some of the liberties away from the individual wage-earner, and that health insurance would take more; that the tendency of health insurance would be to pauperize the workers; that health insurance was not suited to American needs; that health insurance abroad was economically unsuccessful; that its cost was prohibitive; that it was an encouragement of malingering, and that self-respecting labor did not desire it."[28]

Toward the end of the pamphlet, once again warning of the dangers to America of adopting anything resembling Bismarck's single-payer national health insurance system, Hoffman summarized:

> *The German experiment in paternalism and coercion sounds the most convincing note of warning to other industrial countries, where under free institutions, under conditions of voluntary service, savings and self-sacrifice, infinitely better and more lasting results have been achieved.*
>
> *It is devoutly to be hoped that the warning will be heeded by the American people and that they will develop a strong and thoroughly effective opposition to any and every tendency towards autocracy, paternalism and coercion, under the plea of Social Insurance as inherently hostile and fatal to our traditional conceptions of personal and political liberty in a democracy.*[29]

Hoffman's writing and speeches shook America's political systems, particularly as this German-born "man of science" warned of the dire consequences to American liberty and democracy represented by universal health insurance.

In 1918, John R. Commons—one of the AALL's cofounders—wrote that almost all the nation's anti–compulsory health insurance propaganda "originates from one source; all of the ammunition, all of the facts and statistics that may come across, no matter who gives them to you, will be found to go back to the Prudential Insurance Co. of America, and to Mr. Frederick L. Hoffman."[30]

Prudential paid to transport Hoffman all across America, from media events to congressional hearings to a trip to England to document the horrors of their National Health Service system, which had gone into effect in 1911.

He wrote from London, in a widely read paper, that because of the British National Insurance Act, "The fine spirit of the English working classes, at one time the finest people of that type in the world, is gone, entirely gone."[31]

Historian Beatrix Hoffman wrote, "His agitation was tireless, his influence widespread. . . . His reputation as an expert allowed Hoffman to participate in the deliberations of the health insurance commissions of Illinois, Wisconsin, and Connecticut, and to successfully persuade commission members to vote against the plan."

In 1920, in large part because of Prudential's efforts and Hoffman's warnings, California's voters resoundingly turned down a voter initiative in that state to provide health insurance, and, although New York's Senate passed the bill, it died in committee in the Assembly.

While the AALL continued to campaign for state-funded health insurance until their dissolution in 1946, they never again gained enough traction to get their proposal before any state legislatures or the US Congress.

Having succeeded in killing state-funded health insurance, Hoffman, in the later 1920s, turned his attention back to his theory that Black people would eventually die out, joining the

Eugenics Research Association (whose work was later used by Hitler to justify racial separation and his "final solution").

In 1929, Hoffman asserted, in the African American publication *Opportunity*, that "the white race is almost solely responsible . . . for the health progress which the South has made during the last generation" and that Black people moving in large numbers into cities would "lead to a thoroughly unwholesome state of affairs which unquestionably will express itself in course of time in a lower birth rate and a higher death rate."[32]

Hoffman's influence lasted long past his death in 1946 (which satisfied his stated desire to live long enough to see FDR out of office). As late as 1984, according to reporting in the *Wall Street Journal*, Prudential was still collecting premiums from African Americans that were "in some instances more than a third higher" than those paid by whites.[33]

PART THREE

The Modern Fight for a Human Right to Healthcare

Is Healthcare a Right or a Privilege?

Although there are a variety of ways and means by which Americans can acquire healthcare or health insurance, the bottom line of it all is quite binary: access to quality healthcare is either a *right* or a *privilege*.

The answer to this debate informs the entire spectrum of policy solutions and systems to fund and deliver healthcare.

It's the largest question of all: does human nature or high-functioning political culture require that healthcare be a birthright of citizenship or even of humanity, or do we need to hold out healthcare and other essential services as if they were a carrot before a horse to get people to pull the cart of an economically and politically functional society?

And does treating healthcare as a thing to be earned rather than a birthright actually help a society or country in any way? Does it increase worker productivity? Does it lead to a healthier population? Does it incentivize people in any positive way whatsoever?

Conservatives say that people should have full access to quality healthcare only if they earn it. They have a variety of rationalizations, justifications, and historical examples to support their hypothesis. Most of these go something like this:

- People won't value things they're given.

- People will abuse access to healthcare given a chance.

- People won't work if they're not afraid of getting sick.

- Society can't afford the cost of insuring everybody.
- Supporting the weak and frail will degrade the human gene pool.
- Society has no obligation to care for those who won't care for themselves.
- I have no responsibility to pay for somebody else's healthcare.
- I don't want to subsidize other people's obesity, smoking, or other moral failing.
- I already pay too much in taxes.
- "Freedom" means I don't have obligations to "society" (Margaret Thatcher famously said, "There's no such thing as 'society'; there's only a collection of individuals").
- America never did this before and we got along fine.
- Philanthropists and churches should be taking care of the needy, not me.
- This is socialism!
- What's next? I have to pay for people's housing, too?

These objections, at their core, argue that we're each responsible for ourselves, but none of us are really responsible for anybody or everybody else. Just slightly changing the question, though, immediately shows the logical and moral fallacy of these statements.

Instead of asking, "Should your tax money go to provide society (including yourself) with healthcare, or should you alone be responsible for taking care of sickness?" try asking, "Should your tax money go to provide society (including yourself) with a fire department, or should you be responsible for putting it out if your house catches on fire?"

While the first organized municipal fire department was described in a 1690 book by Jan van der Heyden, it was largely for wealthy people and mostly privately funded.[1] By the 1830s, insurance companies had started funding fire departments, but they only showed up when the home of a policyholder was on fire.

The problem they encountered was that fires have an obnoxious tendency to move from one wooden building to the next—much like infectious diseases in people.

Various American communities experimented with paid, private fire departments, but the optics of driving a fire truck past a house that hadn't paid into the department and letting it burn down were bad—and, again, fires often don't just stay where they started. (There are still some private fire departments in the United States, although the biggest are in large high-end gated or private residential communities and supplement local fire departments.)

All but the most hard-core libertarian ideologues would agree that publicly funded fire departments that take care of everything and anything that may catch on fire are a good idea.

Thus, the follow-up question is always, "Isn't your body more important than your house? Why should we all contribute to protect your house when it catches on fire, but not contribute to protect your body when it (metaphorically) does?"

In this section, we will see the history of the fight for healthcare as a *right* and how it has been undermined simultaneously by well-funded libertarian and "free market" think tanks, along with America's history of white supremacy. America's current healthcare system is simultaneously a *product* of white supremacy and systemic racism and an *instrument* for upholding those same institutions.

Why Social Security Doesn't Already Include a Right to Healthcare

President Franklin Roosevelt made Frances Perkins our first female labor secretary, letting her confront an issue she well knew and giving her an opportunity to push for a national healthcare system.

As a working woman, she was often ignored or treated with massive disrespect and even outright scorn. Her husband and daughter both suffered from serious bipolar disorder, and wags in the press accused her of having an affair with Eleanor Roosevelt—"How else," they would ask, "could a woman possibly end up in the Cabinet of the most powerful man in the world?"

Her first contact with real poverty was as a new college student, and she wrote of that experience, "From the time I was in college I was horrified at the work that many women and children had to do in factories. There were absolutely no effective laws that regulated the number of hours they were permitted to work. There were no provisions which guarded their health nor adequately looked after their compensation in case of injury. Those things seemed very wrong. I was young and was inspired with the idea of reforming, or at least doing what I could, to help change those abuses."[2]

In 1905, when she was working with the poor as a student in Chicago, she wrote, "I had to do something about unnecessary hazards to life, unnecessary poverty. It was sort of up to me."[3]

She became a crusader for workers' rights and safety after America watched dozens of young women and girls throw themselves to their deaths in New York City when the Triangle Shirtwaist Factory caught fire with the workers locked inside.

As her biography on the Frances Perkins Center's website says,

> *When, in February, 1933, President-elect Roosevelt asked Frances Perkins to serve in his cabinet as Secretary of Labor, she outlined for him a set of policy priorities she would pursue: a 40-hour work week; a minimum wage; unemployment compensation; worker's compensation; abolition of child labor; direct federal aid to the states for unemployment relief; Social Security; a revitalized federal employment service; and universal health insurance.*
>
> *She made it clear to Roosevelt that his agreement with these priorities was a condition of her joining his cabinet. Roosevelt said he endorsed them all, and Frances Perkins became the first woman in the nation to serve in a Presidential cabinet.*[4]

While Perkins deserves much credit for the authorship and passage of many of the New Deal programs, she was empowered by the loud demands of people and the growing strength of worker unions at the time.

One part that she fought hard for, but never lived to see put into law in the United States, was universal health insurance coverage. Social Security was always intended to be a cradle-to-grave program of coverage, and in Perkins's mind that included health insurance coverage for everyone through the government.

Roosevelt and Perkins were slandered as communists and socialists for their economic proposals, but like Bismarck before them, the Roosevelt administration persuaded lawmakers to implement new social programs as a matter of *national security*.

The Depression had already forced Congress's hand to pass a series of socially and economically progressive emergency relief measures. In January 1935, FDR introduced the administration's plan for economic security to Congress, much of it aimed to make many of the temporary emergency measures permanent.

On February 25, 1935, Perkins spoke at length about the program in a national radio address, first explaining, "The process of recovery is not a simple one. We cannot be satisfied merely with makeshift arrangements which will tide us over the present emergencies. We must devise plans that will not merely alleviate the ills of today, but will prevent, as far as it is humanly possible to do so, their recurrence in the future. The task of recovery is inseparable from the fundamental task of social reconstruction."[5]

She went on to lay out exactly how their plan addressed the nation's economic security: "Our program deals with safeguards against unemployment, with old-age security, with maternal aid and aid to crippled and dependent children and public health services."

But she recognized that public health *services* didn't include public health *insurance*, which she hoped to see presented as a concrete plan in some near future: "Another major subject—health insurance—is dealt with briefly in the report of the Committee on Economic Security, but without any definite recommendations. Fortunate in having secured the cooperation of the medical and other professions directly concerned, the committee is working on a plan for health insurance which will be reported later in the year. Our present program calls for the extension of existing public health services to meet conditions accentuated by the depression. Similarly, the provisions for maternal aid and aid to dependent and crippled children are not new departures, but rather the extension and amplification of safeguards which for a number of years have been a recognized part of public responsibility."[6]

As the Frances Perkins Center notes, the American Medical Association mobilized such intense opposition to her plan for universal health insurance that it threatened to scuttle the entire Social Security Act from becoming law.[7]

Author Adam Cohen clarified to Amy Goodman in 2009, "She really was the conscience of the New Deal in many ways . . . she chaired the Social Security committee. And she wanted it to go further . . . to include national health insurance, but the AMA (American Medical Association), even back then, was very strong and opposed it. And she and a couple other progressives on the committee said, you know, 'We better just settle for what we can get.' They didn't want to lose the whole Social Security program."[8]

Perkins herself wrote in an introduction to Edwin E. Witte's book *Development of the Social Security Act* that national health insurance "would have killed the whole Social Security Act if it had been pressed at that time."[9]

By August 14, 1935, despite a report having been commissioned, nothing was moving forward with the plan for national health insurance. Historian Jaap Kooijman wrote in *Presidential Studies Quarterly* that Assistant Secretary of Labor Arthur Altmeyer asked Roosevelt's press secretary Stephen Early what he should do with the health insurance report. According to Kooijman, Altmeyer "believed that the report described a 'practical program' that could challenge the opposition." Early responded that it was an "old report—and the president hopes no publicity will be given it. Just forget about it."

The report was forwarded to the Social Security Board for further study, but shortly thereafter Roosevelt signaled that he had no intention of promoting the plan further.

Kooijman describes the dedication of a partially federally funded medical center in Jersey City, New Jersey. When Roosevelt spoke, he declared that "we must do more, much more to help the small-income families in time of sickness," but then he conceded to the gathered medical professionals that "the overwhelming majority of the doctors of the Nation want medicine kept out of politics. On occasions in the past attempts have been made to put medicine into politics. Such attempts have always failed and always will fail."[10]

Frances Perkins lived long enough to see two more major attempts to create a universal health insurance system, first as part of FDR's "Second Bill of Rights," and then when President Harry Truman similarly failed. She died on May 14, 1965, just two and a half months before Medicare was signed into law on July 30, 1965.

But if FDR was right and doctors wanted "medicine kept out of politics," how did other developed English-speaking countries like Canada and those in the United Kingdom get their universal healthcare programs?

Healthcare to Defeat Fascism

As far as the press knew, President Franklin D. Roosevelt, along with a small entourage, had taken the presidential yacht, the *Sequoia*, on a 10-day fly-fishing trip off the coast of northern New England in early August 1941. In reality, he'd left the yacht on August 5 to board the *USS Augusta*, just off the coast of Newfoundland, Canada.[11] It was a Northampton-class heavy cruiser that later would be the flagship for the D-Day landings.

The United States had not yet entered the war—that would happen when the Japanese attacked Pearl Harbor on December 7—but there were urgent questions to be answered for the future, particularly if fascism was defeated.

The *Augusta* met the *HMS Prince of Wales*, a British battleship that would later be sunk by a Japanese torpedo off the coast of Singapore, but that day it was secretly carrying British prime minister Winston Churchill.

Sunday morning, August 10, the two leaders met on the fantail of the *Prince of Wales* and sat through a church service with the ship's crew; Churchill himself had selected the hymns, working from the obscure up to a finale with "Onward Christian Soldiers."

Churchill later said that he'd chosen that particular hymn to highlight the service because "I felt that this was no vain presumption, but that we had the right to feel that we are serving a cause for the sake of which a trumpet has sounded from on high."

After the service, he concluded that the choice was both wise and important.

"When I looked upon that densely packed congregation of fighting men of the same language, of the same faith, of the same fundamental laws, of the same ideals," Churchill said, "it swept across me that here was the only hope, but also the sure hope, of saving the world from measureless degradation."[12]

Nobody knows for sure what was discussed during Roosevelt and Churchill's several days of meetings. American fascists like Charles Lindbergh, who were agitating against America coming to Europe's defense against Hitler, would have met public news of the meeting with outrage; they and their Republican allies in Congress were constantly accusing FDR of a secret plan to enter the war.

Republican opposition to challenging Hitler was so strong, in fact, that America's then-top-selling novelist, Rex Stout (creator of the Nero Wolfe detective series, which sold over 70 million copies), published a book made up entirely of floor speeches from American fascist sympathizers such as Representative Hamilton Fish, Republican of New York, who declared at an America First rally, "Colonel Lindbergh was right when he said in one of his recent speeches, 'Let us stop this hysterical chatter about calamity and invasion.'"[13]

Fish said, on the floor of Congress on June 22, 1940, "Let us have an end to the secret diplomacy and the secret commitments of President Roosevelt . . . Roosevelt alarmed the nation. . . . We have more to fear from the warmakers from within than from our enemies without."[14]

Stout's book *The Illustrious Dunderheads*, today a classic and a collector's item, illustrates what a struggle FDR faced against America's right wing.

The Atlantic Charter was a short document sent by telegraph from FDR's warship to Washington, DC, on August 14, 1941. Its purpose was to define what the developed world would need to do *after* the war was over to prevent the rise of another fascistic regime among other democratic nations.[15]

It said explicitly that neither the United States nor Great Britain was trying to seize any country's territory, that Nazi-occupied countries should have "self-government restored to [them]," and that "all nations" should work toward "securing, for all, improved labor standards, economic advancement and social security."[16]

When the nearly 200 legislators that Stout quotes later learned what FDR and Churchill had been planning, all hell broke loose.

Roosevelt briefed Congress on August 21 and responded to the GOP outrage that he'd dared meet with Churchill in secret and negotiate a document that "promoted socialism" by metaphorically tweaking their noses.

"There isn't any copy of *The Atlantic Charter*, so far as I know," he said. "I haven't got one. The British haven't got one. The nearest thing you will get is [from] the radio operator on *Augusta* and *Prince of Wales*. That's the nearest thing you will come to it. . . . There was no formal document."[17]

Nonetheless, *The Atlantic Charter* set off a firestorm that eventually led to Britain—and almost every other country in Europe—developing a universal national healthcare program. Its core premise was that fascist governments, being focused on the rights and income of corporations and the very wealthy (the most common definition of fascism then was "a merger of state and business interests, combined with belligerent nationalism"), produced increasing levels of misery among their people as wages slipped and workers' rights were suppressed.

That misery, while causing many to openly ask for strongman rule, could effectively be answered by a government that actually met the needs of its people. Social welfare programs, including a national healthcare program, in other words, were the best way to prevent the rise of fascism in a democratic republic.

In the United States, *New York Post* columnist Samuel Grafton published an article stating that "[t]he English press began to debate the need for an 'economic bill of rights,' to defeat Hitlerism in the world forever by establishing minimum standards of housing, food, education and medical care, along with free speech, free press and free worship."

FDR's main speechwriter, Sam Rosenman, wrote that a copy of Grafton's article was in the file that Roosevelt had compiled in preparation for his later "Four Freedoms" speech, which explicitly called for healthcare in the United States to be legally a universal American *right* rather than a mere *privilege*.[18]

The Atlantic Charter also led to a September 1942 publication by the US National Resources Planning Board titled *After the War—Toward Security: Freedom From Want*. The pamphlet noted that "without social and economic security there can be no true guarantee of freedom" because having a strong social safety net including provisions for the nation's health was, "indeed, a fundamental part of national defense."[19]

Across the Atlantic, just after America joined Britain to fight fascist Germany, Robert M. Barrington-Ward, editor of the *London Times*, wrote Churchill in April 1942 that it was time for Britain to take up "the essential purpose of the *Charter*."

"They are aims which will more and more obliterate the distinctions once possible between domestic and foreign policy," Barrington-Ward wrote, echoing the idea that the best way to fight fascism was to remove the worker insecurity that often brought it to power (as had happened in Germany in the wreckage after World War I). "The realization of the *Charter*," he added, "can and must begin at home."[20]

And the "aims" that so animated Barrington-Ward? "The fundamental demand of the peace-makers," he wrote, "from uncounted millions of mankind, will be for welfare and security."

Two months later, in November 1942, Sir William Beveridge presented a report to the British Parliament summarizing how that nation might most effectively "banish poverty and want" from its shores and prevent forever a fascist rise in the UK.

The Beveridge Report:
The British Plan for Defense and Welfare

The Beveridge Report, while not well known in the United States, is as familiar to every British schoolchild as Lincoln's Gettysburg Address is to Americans. Beveridge saw himself as a revolutionary in the mold of FDR—taking bold steps to solve big problems, paramount among them the widespread lack of access to healthcare.

"A revolutionary moment in the world's history is a time for revolutions, not for patching," he wrote about his report.[21]

At the time, the UK's health and insurance system resembled today's in the United States. There was means-tested help for poor people, along with competing insurance companies and competing hospital systems, while doctors and pharmaceutical companies pretty much charged whatever they could get away with.

Beveridge pointed out that Britain's social welfare system, including supports for healthcare, was a "complex of disconnected administrative organs, proceeding on different principles, doing invaluable service but at a cost in money and trouble and anomalous treatment of identical problems for which there is no justification."[22]

Beveridge wrote that there were then "five giants on the road" blocking progress toward a more just society, including "Want, Disease, Ignorance, Squalor, and Idleness."[23]

When the report was submitted to Parliament, a huge debate broke out, with conservatives like Brendan Bracken suggesting that it should be suppressed and never officially published.

Sir Kingsley Wood, the chancellor of the exchequer, complained that following Beveridge's recommendations would hit Britain—even after the war—with "an impracticable financial commitment."

Nonetheless, with Churchill's emphatic support, the cabinet voted on November 26 to publish the *Report* on December 2, 1942.

Beveridge's report hit Britain like a thunderclap. As recounted in *Welfare States and Societies in the Making*, "The

MOI Home Intelligence reported that the plan had been 'welcomed with almost universal approval by people of all shades of opinion and by all sections of the community,' and that it was seen as the first step towards postwar reconstruction and as 'the first real attempt to put into practice the talk about the new world.' . . . A British Institute of Public Opinion Report based on a sample taken in the fortnight after publication of the White Paper found that 95 per cent of the public had heard about it; that there was 'great interest in it,' most markedly 'among poorer people.' The greatest criticism, the BIPO found, was that the proposed old-age pensions were not high enough. 'There was overwhelming agreement that the plan should be put into effect.'"[24] Amazingly, Churchill's own conservative Tories were among the most anxious to fascism-proof Britain with a strong social welfare system, including a national health service. "The Tory Reform Committee, consisting of 45 Conservative MPs, demanded the founding of a Ministry of Social Security immediately."[25]

The next spring, the war was still going on, worse than ever in some respects. Nonetheless, Churchill and Parliament continued hard at work on implementing Beveridge's vision for a national healthcare system. He gave a speech broadcast live by the BBC on March 21, 1943, which he titled "After the War," promising that once the war was over, there would be "a four-year plan" that would put into place a national "compulsory" (everybody in) health insurance program for the country.

"I have been prominently connected with all these schemes of national compulsory organized thrift from the time when I brought my friend Sir William Beveridge into the public service thirty-five years ago," Churchill said, then mentioning Lloyd George's social security program for widows, orphans, and people over 65, which had been put into place 18 years earlier with Churchill's help.

"The time is now ripe for another great advance," he summarized, "and any one can see what large savings there will be in administration once the whole process of insurance becomes unified, compulsory and national. Here is a real opportunity for what I once called 'bringing the magic of averages to the rescue of the millions,' therefore, you must rank me and my colleagues as strong partisans of national compulsory insurance for all classes, for all purposes, from the cradle to the grave."[26]

Churchill won World War II but lost the British election of 1945, so it was Prime Minister Clement Attlee, with the help of his health minister, Aneurin Bevan, who put the National Health Service into place.

According to *Historic UK*, "This project was said to be based on three ideas which Bevan expressed in the launch on 5th July 1948. These essential values were, firstly, that the services helped everyone; secondly, healthcare was free and finally, that care would be provided based on need rather than ability to pay."[27]

Churchill had promised that "every preparation . . . will be made with the utmost energy . . . so that when the moment comes everything will be ready."[28] He hadn't failed.

In 1948, President Harry Truman tried unsuccessfully to pass the national single-payer healthcare system that FDR had proposed four years earlier, but Truman was defeated in the effort by Republicans in Congress.

These failed attempts in the United States did not stop Canadians from picking up the idea.

How Canada Won a Right to Healthcare

It's nearly impossible to disentangle universal healthcare from basic human rights; healthcare is the ultimate right-to-life issue. But it can also be expedient for conservative politicians who would otherwise not be inclined to "give" citizens free healthcare.

The arch-conservative Otto von Bismarck brought universal healthcare to Germany, and the hard-core conservative Winston Churchill first proposed the British National Health Service in his March 21, 1943, speech (saying it must cover all Britons "from cradle to grave").[29] Closer to home, the Canadian national Medicare system was taken national with legislation supported by Canada's conservative prime minister, John Diefenbaker.[30]

But in every case, and consistently around the world, it was a progressive, grassroots sentiment that brought universal healthcare to the fore.

Tommy Douglas was, in many ways, the Bernie Sanders of Canada (albeit in the 1940s and 1950s), from his childhood experiences that turned him into a progressive activist to his untiring decades of work to make healthcare a right, rather than a privilege.

Healthcare—or the lack of it—informed Douglas's own journey.

In 1910, when he was six years old, he injured his leg, and because his family lacked access to a doctor or hospital, it healed badly. The wound continued to hurt and fester until, four years later, the infection worked its way deep into his leg bone.

In desperation, his parents took him to a doctor, who said that surgery to open the leg and clean out the wound would be too expensive and complex for the family to afford; he'd have to amputate the leg. By happenstance, another surgeon at the hospital "took an interest" in the case and offered to do the surgery for free if his medical students could watch, a deal the Douglas family made, saving the leg.[31]

"Had I been a rich man's son," Douglas wrote, "the services of the finest surgeons would have been available. As an iron molder's boy, I almost had my leg amputated before chance intervened and a specialist cured me without thought of a fee."[32]

In 1919, Douglas was a teenager living with his parents in Winnipeg. A huge workers' protest for better wages and safer working conditions had formed on a major street a block or so away, and Douglas climbed to his rooftop to check it out.

As he watched, a large contingent of police arrived, pulled out their weapons, and shot 20 of the peaceful protesters, killing two and severely injuring most of the rest. The young Douglas was horrified; watching those men writhe in pain and die was, for him, a life-changing experience.

A decade later, he was working as the pastor of the Calvary Baptist Church in Weyburn, Saskatchewan, still horrified by working people's lack of access to healthcare.

"I buried two young men in their 30s with young families who died because there was no doctor readily available and they hadn't the money to get proper care," he wrote at the time.[33]

And then another labor strike came to his door, this time miners in his little town protesting dangerous working conditions, brutal bosses, and lousy pay. Douglas organized his church to collect blankets and food for the striking workers, who were essentially camping in the streets and public places as they conducted their protest.

After a few days of this, as Douglas was passing out food, the police again showed up, firing into the crowd and killing three of the miners on the spot.

The experience led Douglas, in 1934, to join the Co-operative Commonwealth Federation (CCF), a political party advocating democratic socialism for Canada. The next year, he ran for parliament on their ticket and won a seat in Canada's federal House of Commons.

After nine years of working without success at the federal level to bring about healthcare for all Canadians, Douglas gave up and returned to Saskatchewan, running for premier (what we'd call governor) and winning the seat at the age of 39.

In 1947, he succeeded in passing numerous progressive reforms, including forcing the University of Saskatchewan to open a school of medicine to ensure that the state would have a good supply of doctors and other medical professionals.

Only Saskatchewan's larger cities had electricity when Douglas was elected; within a few years he'd extended it to every rural area in the province. He passed a law requiring two weeks of paid vacation for workers and a bill of rights ending legal racial discrimination. He put into place a state-run low-cost auto insurance program and a law guaranteeing the "right of assembly" so that police could never again legally attack or kill strikers.

The formerly backwater province, as a result of Douglas's

reforms (raising taxes on the very wealthy, seizing private electric and water utilities and turning their profits over to the state, and taking over the lumber industry), had one of the strongest economies in the entire nation.

In 1958, John Diefenbaker became prime minister of Canada as he formed the first conservative government to run that nation since Prime Minister R. B. Bennett had given up on politics and fled to England in 1935.

The next year, in Saskatchewan, Douglas proposed a provincewide program he called Medicare, charging $5 a month and providing full medical, hospital, and dental coverage for all Saskatchewan residents of all ages.

In the lead-up to the vote, the Canadian Medical Association (CMA) and the American Medical Association (AMA) worked together with insurance companies and Saskatchewan's conservative elite to fight Douglas's proposal tooth and nail.

They raised a war chest unseen in previous Canadian politics, flooding the airwaves and newspapers with warnings of "Socialism!" and delivering detailed indictments of "government-controlled medicine" to every home. Provincewide, local chambers of commerce and boards of trade held public rallies charging Douglas and advocates of Medicare with communist leanings, saying they'd destroy the very fabric of the nation.[34]

One anti-Medicare propaganda piece said that Douglas's proposal would drive so many physicians out of Saskatchewan that "[t]hey'll have to fill up the profession with the garbage of Europe; some of the European doctors who come out here are so bad we wonder if they ever practiced medicine."[35]

Nonetheless, Douglas prevailed and Saskatchewan got Medicare. And the people loved it.

Medicare and Douglas's popularity in Saskatchewan inspired Diefenbaker to work with him to bring Saskatchewan's Medicare program to the entire country, with the first successful federal legislation to accomplish this introduced in 1961, splitting the costs roughly 50/50 between federal and provincial governments.

Again, the CMA, AMA, chambers of commerce, and other business organizations launched a campaign, this time nationwide, of vilification similar to the earlier one in Saskatchewan, highlighted by a 23-day nationwide doctors' strike in 1962 in protest of "socialized medicine," along with "racial slurs, red-baiting, acts of violence and threats of blood in the streets."[36]

The Keep Our Doctors committee—a 1960s astroturf version of the Koch brothers' 2009 Tea Party—joined in, with the Billy Graham of Canada, a right-wing priest named Athol Murray, telling a nationwide radio audience, "This thing may break into violence and bloodshed any day now, and God help us if it doesn't!"

Nonetheless, Canadians could see with their own eyes how well it worked in Douglas's Saskatchewan: a national Medicare system was fully implemented when the last province ratified it in 1966, making Douglas a national hero and helping Diefenbaker maintain his hold on federal politics until he died in office in 1979.

It hadn't been easy for Douglas. The Royal Canadian Mounted Police (their federal police force, like the United

States' FBI) harassed and spied on him for decades, compiling an official file with more than 1,100 pages.

He was burned in effigy numerous times, threatened with death, and accused by the American Medical Association and their Canadian brethren of communist leanings, alternately depicted in conservative media as a "Nazi, Stalinist or both."[37]

Despite it all, today every Canadian has comprehensive health insurance provided by that nation's Medicare program, and Tommy Douglas, "the father of Canadian Medicare," has repeatedly been selected as the most popular Canadian in Canadian history.

LBJ Takes It to Reagan and the Doctors

America followed a somewhat different path.

On June 13, 1961, President John F. Kennedy gave a speech proposing what we today call Medicare. "I do not know any problem or remedy more obvious which now faces the Congress of the United States," Kennedy said, speaking of elderly Americans on fixed incomes without health insurance.

"Now, the program we suggested," Kennedy said, "will provide that [the working person] will set aside during his working years an average of $13 a year, not a burden for anyone employed, $13 a year. And that man and woman will know when they are over 65 that they will never be a burden upon their children and never be a charity case upon the national government."

It was a sweeping and classic Kennedy proposal, on the order of sending a man to the moon, that, four years later, President

Johnson would remind Americans of as he used Kennedy's memory to shame legislators into voting for Medicare.

"There isn't a country in Western Europe that didn't do what we are doing 50 years ago or 40 years ago . . . ," Kennedy said. "We are not suggesting something radical and new or violent. We are not suggesting that the government come between the doctor and his patient. We are suggesting what every other major, developed, intelligent country did for its people a generation ago."

He closed the speech with a simple challenge: "I think it is time the United States caught up."[38]

In response, the all-white American Medical Association hired B-movie actor Ronald Reagan to record a chilling warning, one that defeated Kennedy's initiative. Reagan cast the debate not as one about healthcare but as a battle between democracy and socialism, then the feared province of the Union of Soviet Socialist Republics, the USSR.

"[T]his threat is with us," Reagan warned in a grave voice, "and, at the moment, is more imminent" than at any time in the past.

Embracing his version of Frederick Hoffman's 1920s warnings about the dangers of the "Prussian way" of single-payer medicine, Reagan said, "One of the traditional methods of imposing statism or socialism on a people has been by way of medicine. It's very easy to disguise a medical program as a humanitarian project. Most people are a little reluctant to oppose anything that suggests medical care for people who possibly can't afford it."

Dismissing the idea that elderly people in America were experiencing a healthcare crisis, he said Kennedy's program "is presented in the idea of a great emergency that millions of our senior citizens are unable to provide needed medical care. . . . Now the advocates of this bill, when you try to oppose it, challenge you on an emotional basis. They say, 'What would you do, throw these poor old people out to die without medical attention?' That's ridiculous; and, of course, no one's advocated it."

But Reagan was, indeed, advocating that seniors continue to die from lack of access to healthcare. And all in the name of fighting those evil socialists and communists.

The 33⅓ rpm long-form recording was distributed by the AMA to doctors and conservatives all across the country; my dad, a mere foot soldier in the GOP, had a copy of it that he played for our entire family.

At its end, Reagan called on us all to send letters to our members of Congress to "demand the continuation of our traditional free enterprise system."

"If you don't," he warned, "this program, I promise you, will pass just as surely as the sun will come up tomorrow; and behind it will come other federal programs that will invade every area of freedom as we have known it in this country. Until, one day, as [former Socialist Party candidate for president] Norman Thomas said, we will awake to find that we have socialism."

I can still remember my dad quoting Reagan's last line: "If you don't do this and I don't do it, one of these days you and I are going to spend our sunset years telling our children, and our children's children, what it once was like in America when men were free."[39]

It wasn't until 2008 that the AMA formally apologized to Black doctors for almost two centuries of white-supremacy-fueled opposition to integrating the nation's medical system, and even then the president of the AMA at the time wasn't willing to do the job; it fell to Ronald M. Davis, the association's "immediate past president."[40]

While America's white doctors were worried about Medicare, they were even more hysterical about having to work with Black doctors and treat Black patients, which universal coverage like Medicare would require. Reagan's recording helped the all-white AMA fight back Kennedy's "socialism," but only for a few years.

The month before Medicare passed Congress, the 10,000-plus physicians of the Ohio Medical Association voted for a boycott if it became law. Shortly thereafter, a group of AMA doctors set out for Washington, DC, to fight the bill.

AFL-CIO president George Meany, a big supporter of Medicare, was worried. He went to the White House to share his concerns about the incoming doctors with President Johnson.

Robert Dallek, in his 1998 biography of LBJ, *Flawed Giant: Lyndon Johnson and His Times*, recounts the conversation.

> *"George, have you ever fed chickens?" LBJ asked George Meany.*
>
> *"No," Meany answered.*
>
> *"Well," Johnson said, "chickens are real dumb. They eat and eat and never stop. Why, they start shitting at the same time they're eating and before you know it, they're knee deep in their own shit. Well, the AMA's the same. They've been eating and eating and now they're knee deep in their own shit and everybody knows it. They won't be able to stop anything."*[41]

Nonetheless, the AMA's opposition to Medicare was problematic for Johnson. He didn't have the easy target of hospitals he could strong-arm with a single organization representing over 100,000 doctors, the way he'd manipulated the leadership of the AMA.

Medicare Part A paid for hospital expenses, and Medicare Part B reimbursed doctors for their services; both required compliance with Title VI of the Civil Rights Act.

But integrating doctors' offices wasn't as easy as integrating hospitals, because their billing and practices were scattered all over, and the AMA continued (while giving lip service to integration) to countenance segregation.

In 1965, an integrated crowd of 200 protesters picketed the American Medical Association's annual convention, calling for integration of that organization. The next year, 400 people showed up to demonstrate.[42]

When the contingent of AMA doctors that George Meany had worried about showed up at the White House with just two days to go before President Johnson would have to either sign or veto Medicare, LBJ performed one of the political magic tricks that had made him famous.

The LBJ Presidential Library quotes Joseph Califano, who later wrote up the story in *The Triumph and Tragedy of Lyndon Johnson: The White House Years.*

> *Sitting around the cabinet table, the AMA officials waited politely for Johnson to say something as he settled into his chair. The President took his time, gazing at their cold stares. Then he talked about the need for physicians in Vietnam to help serve the civilian population. Would the AMA help? Could it get doctors to rotate in and out of*

Vietnam for a few months? . . . He got the reply he expected. Of course, the AMA would start a program immediately, the doctors responded, almost in unison.

"Get a couple of reporters in here," Johnson said.

The President described the AMA Vietnam medical program, heaping praise on the doctors present, but the reporters wanted to know about Medicare. Would the doctors support the Medicare program?

"These men are going to get doctors to go to Vietnam where they might be killed," Johnson said indignantly. "Medicare is the law of the land. Of course they'll support the law of the land."

LBJ turned to Dr. James Appel, the AMA president. "Tell him," he said. "You tell him."

Dr. Appel told them. Two days later, LBJ signed the Medicare bill.[43]

Medicare: America's Most Successful Racial Integration Program

The fact that in the entire history of the United States, Medicare was this country's most successful racial integration program is astonishing and virtually unknown to most citizens. The history is amazing.

It's a coincidence that Frederick Hoffman's book *Race Traits and Tendencies of the American Negro* and the Supreme Court's *Plessy v. Ferguson* decision were both issued in 1896, but a coincidence fraught with significance.

That is also the year that Temple University professor David Barton Smith identified as the beginning of the modern US healthcare system, a process he chronicled in considerable detail in his brilliant book *The Power to Heal: Civil Rights, Medicare, and the Struggle to Transform America's Health Care System*.

The "germ theory of disease" work of Louis Pasteur, Joseph Lister, and Robert Koch in the 1860s and 1870s was only beginning to gain wide acceptance in medical practice in America in the 1890s. Antibiotics wouldn't become available in a meaningful way until the 1930s, so the need for a "clean" environment for surgery and other medical procedures drove the development of hospitals all across the country.[44]

The 1896 *Plessy* decision gave those hospitals all the power of law they needed to strictly enforce racial segregation, resulting in generations of African American citizens dying at home for lack of medical treatment or having to settle for levels of care reminiscent of the days of slavery.

As of 1964, things hadn't changed that much. Black people were routinely denied entrance to most hospitals, even when in labor or suffering from severe trauma, and when they were admitted, it was often into cramped basement quarters where they'd have to wait for hours—sometimes days—until doctors had attended to all the white patients upstairs.

When the Supreme Court ordered desegregation of America's schools in the 1954 *Brown v. Board of Education* decision, they required it be done with "all deliberate speed." "Deliberate," it turned out, was a word open to interpretation, and America's schools are *still* highly segregated, with today's private school sector almost entirely segregated.

Thus, when the Civil Rights Act made its way through Congress and was signed into law by President Johnson in 1964, everybody figured it would be a replay of *Brown*: full of sound and fury but, in reality, signifying nothing.

However, the following year a small group of men in the federal government—including LBJ; Social Security commissioner Robert Ball; John Gardner, secretary of Health, Education, and Welfare; Wilbur Cohen, undersecretary of Health, Education, and Welfare; and Surgeon General William Stewart—entered into a conspiracy of sorts with a disparate group of civil rights activists, including the Southern Christian Leadership Conference (SCLC), the Student Nonviolent Coordinating Committee (SNCC), the National Urban League, and the NAACP (among others), to undertake the largest, most consequential, and fastest integration of healthcare in all of American history.

The tool they used was the Medicare law that was passed in 1965, along with the fact, downplayed to a whisper by LBJ and his allies, that it required compliance with the Civil Rights Act of 1964.

Medicare "Inspectors" Defeat Goldwater's Racists

Title VI of the Civil Rights Act required that any business receiving federal assistance of any sort must be integrated, but hospitals basically laughed at that provision, just as most schools had done a decade earlier.

The November 1964 issue of *Hospitals*, the publication of the American Hospital Association, carried an article by the administrator of Methodist Hospital, in Gary, Indiana, unearthed and quoted by David Barton Smith in *The Power to Heal*.[45]

Noting that "the historical right of medicine [is] to make the patient's wellbeing its most important concern," the article says that when "patients have predetermined convictions on racial matters, efforts to force changes in them at the time of illness can be detrimental to their medical care."

Couching the entire argument in the frame of white patients' potential to freak out if they're in a hospital room, ward, or floor with Black patients, the article asserts that maintaining segregation "must be [a hospital's] primary consideration." Therefore, of course, "[d]ifficulties will arise in the implementation of the Civil Rights Act."

Just as they had with implementation of *Brown v. Board of Education*.

But the election of 1964, in the wake of JFK's assassination, not only swept LBJ into a full term but also produced a 248–187 Democratic majority in the House and an overwhelming 64–35 Democratic majority in the Senate.

Thus, Medicare passed Congress just a week before the Voting Rights Act did and was signed into law by LBJ on July 30, 1965.[46] Monies appropriated by the Act would be available a mere 11 months later, on July 1, 1966.

But only for fully integrated hospitals.

By the spring of 1966, the co-conspirators were assembled and in action.

On March 4, 1966, Surgeon General Stewart sent a letter to every hospital in the nation stating, "Title VI of the Civil Rights Act of 1964 prohibits discrimination on the basis of race, color or national origin in Federally-assisted programs," adding that "to be eligible" for federal funds, hospitals "must be in compliance with Title VI."[47]

Enclosed with the letter was a form for hospital administrators to fill out and sign, certifying that their hospital no longer practiced racial discrimination. One can imagine them smiling and casually jotting down their signatures, certain that this would go no further than *Brown* had.

"Three weeks later on March 25, 1966," Smith wrote, Martin Luther King Jr. gave a "recruitment pitch for volunteers to join the upcoming battle" before the second annual convention of the Medical Committee for Human Rights. The result was the coalition of civil rights organizations mentioned earlier, drawing together a huge, national pool of volunteers to "inspect" hospitals, both overtly and covertly.

The effort, Smith documented, was mainly led by the NAACP Legal Defense Fund, the National Medical Association (the organization for Black physicians, as the AMA was still fully whites only), and the Medical Committee for Human Rights.[48]

Medicare Ends Segregation in America's Hospitals

Throughout those months after Martin Luther King's March 1966 call for "hospital inspectors" to crisscross the country, the coalition of civil rights groups fanned out, and where they were identified by local hospitals and the local police were notified, things often got ugly.

One inspector had the lug nuts from the front right wheel of her car removed; a snowstorm slowed her car enough that when the wheel fell off, she wasn't seriously injured. Others were arrested on bogus, made-up charges.

An inspector in Mississippi said that his "name was in the telephone directory so it wasn't hard for any of [them] to find out where I lived. . . . I had a five-foot cross burned in my front yard."[49]

Inspectors discovered hospitals all over the country that required their Black employees to hop into empty beds in all-white wards when they knew the inspection was coming. Other hospitals that had all-Black wards would rapidly shuffle Black and white patients, mixing them together, on the day of the visit.

The inspectors would report this back to the Department of Health, Education, and Welfare (HEW), which was charged with implementation of Medicare, and the hospitals quickly learned that such tricks didn't work. The inspectors and HEW were not going to let hospitals move with "all deliberate speed" the way the Eisenhower administration had let schools do.

Even institutions peripheral to hospitals like blood banks discovered that the Johnson administration had no intention whatsoever of backing down.

When it was discovered that the Louisiana Red Cross was still labeling their blood supply as "White" and "Colored," a telegram went to the director of the Louisiana Hospital Association saying that *all* the hospitals in Louisiana would be denied Medicare money if they failed to correct the situation. As Smith wrote, "The Louisiana blood supply was integrated overnight."

In 1964, Republican senator Barry Goldwater of Arizona had spoken in opposition to the Civil Rights Act, saying, "To give genuine effect to the prohibitions of this bill will require the creation of a Federal police force of mammoth proportions."[50]

Goldwater—and his conservative colleagues (including several Southern Democrats who later defected to the GOP over their defense of segregation)—also worried that the Act would, as Goldwater said, "result in the development of an 'informer' psychology in great areas of our national life— neighbors spying on neighbors, workers spying on workers, businessmen spying on businessmen."

Envisioning a white backlash and blood in the streets, Gold-water had warned in his speech on the Senate floor, "These, the federal police force and an 'informer' psychology, are the hallmarks of the police state and landmarks in the destruction of a free society."

But there was big money at stake. In some hospitals, as much as two-thirds of their total billings were for people over 65, and old folks were often indigent. Across the board, America's hospitals were looking at Medicare funds making up as much as half of their total budgets by the end of the 1960s, rescuing an industry that was then deep in trouble.

Medicare payments would begin flowing on July 1, 1966, and the day before, LBJ recorded a televised address to the nation.

"Medicare begins tomorrow...," he said. "Since I signed the historic Medicare act last summer, we have made more extensive preparation to launch this program than for any other peaceful undertaking in our Nation's history.... This program

. . . is a test for all Americans—a test of our willingness to work together. In the past, we have always passed that test. I have no doubt about the future. I believe that July 1, 1966, marks a new day of freedom for our people."[51]

The following day, around 6,500 hospitals and 1,200 home health agencies, now almost fully integrated (there were a few stragglers), became eligible for payments that would rescue their industries.

As Smith wrote, "In four months they transformed the nation's hospitals from our most racially and economically segregated institutions to our most integrated. In four years they changed patterns of use of health services that had persisted for half a century. . . . A profound transformation, now taken for granted, happened almost overnight."[52]

Thus, it wasn't a "mammoth federal police force" or informers (other than the hospital inspectors) who nonviolently integrated the overwhelming majority of the nation's hospitals in less than a single year: it was Medicare.

Which may help explain why white conservatives are so opposed to Medicare for All to this day.

Ted Kennedy's Fight for Expansion

In the 1970s, the entire liberal wing of the Democratic Party was all in on reprising the single-payer universal healthcare program that Harry Truman had tried to get through Congress in the 1940s. Even the nation's biggest unions agreed.

The Campaign for National Health Insurance (CNHI) collected multiple millions of members; it was funded, in large part, by the AFL-CIO and run, day to day, by the Teamsters.

In 1975, Democratic senator Ted Kennedy of Massachusetts was their champion, and he was trying to negotiate some sort of national healthcare plan with President Gerald Ford.

Ford, after all, had called for a national healthcare insurance system in his first address to the nation after Nixon's resignation and his own elevation to the presidency. But when it came time to present a program, Ford defaulted to the GOP's theory that only private industry and the profit motive could do good things.

When, in 1975, the CNHI condemned Ford's idea, which involved having the federal government backstop and subsidize for-profit health insurance companies and add a catastrophic care provision to Medicare, Kennedy pulled out of the negotiations. (It's widely believed that Kennedy had similarly rejected Jimmy Carter's proposal for a national healthcare system during the 1980 Democratic primary election, but that's not the case.)

Kennedy said, "We are the only industrialized nation in the world outside [apartheid] South Africa that does not have universal, comprehensive healthcare insurance. And here, as well as in South Africa, black people are sick twice as often; they receive less care; they die younger; and sooner."[53]

It wasn't the first time a Democratic president or serious contender for the presidency would call for a national healthcare system.

Twenty years earlier, in 1945, President Harry Truman had similarly proposed a single-payer healthcare system:

Under the plan I suggest, our people would continue to get medical and hospital services just as they do now—on the basis of their own voluntary decisions and choices. Our doctors and hospitals would continue to deal with disease with the same professional freedom as now. There would, however, be this all-important difference: whether or not patients get the services they need would not depend on how much they can afford to pay at the time. . . .

None of this is really new. The American people are the most insurance-minded people in the world. They will not be frightened off from health insurance because some people have misnamed it "socialized medicine."

I repeat—what I am recommending is not socialized medicine.

Socialized medicine means that all doctors work as employees of government. The American people want no such system. No such system is here proposed.[54]

The American Medical Association came out with a blistering attack, calling Truman's program "socialized medicine." It was enough to galvanize the Republicans and scare the Democrats.

Millions more Americans would die of lack of healthcare access, and tens of millions would be bankrupted or have their lives and families shattered by medical debt, before the issue was again taken seriously on the national stage in the 2020 Democratic primary election.

PART FOUR

Saving Lives with a Real Healthcare System

Undoing Reaganomics and Reducing Inequality Would Save Lives

At its core, healthcare is about making and keeping people healthy. We think of it in terms of doctors' offices, pharmacies, and hospitals, but it's really all about making and keeping people healthy.

Given that larger frame, there are a number of government policies that have nothing to do with paying doctors' bills but should be an important part of the conversation. Generally, people understand these peripheral issues and policies to include things like taxes that discourage the consumption of tobacco and alcohol, anti-addiction programs, and incentives for people to get more exercise by, for example, bicycling to work.

All of these are important, and many of them move to front and center policy-wise when everybody in a country has a financial stake in the health and well-being of its citizens because everybody is paying into the national healthcare system through their taxes.

But, in terms of bang for the buck, there is one thing that has a greater negative impact on the health of a nation's citizens than any other single policy: economic inequality.

Outside of providing full and free access to healthcare across the board, no other factor has such a broad and sustained influence on the health of a nation's people as does economic inequality.

It's not about poverty. Although the United States has the worst and deepest poverty in the developed world, and poverty has real and negative consequences, inequality affects the health of nearly everybody except the very, very rich in a society.

It's not about spending. The United States accounts for over 40 percent of the entire world's healthcare expenditures (with only a bit more than 4 percent of the world's population) but does not have the world's healthiest or most-long-lived people—far from it. Many much less wealthy countries have much better physical and mental health, even though they spend less than half, per person, of what the United States spends on healthcare.

Inequality is about the difference in the income and/or wealth between a society's richest and poorest members.

Richard Wilkinson and Kate Pickett have spent decades researching inequality, producing a body of work that includes three internationally best-selling books, numerous articles, and a nonprofit called the Equality Trust.[1]

Looking at a wide range of health and social problems across a society, from obesity to children's educational performance to suicide rates, Pickett and Wilkinson found that the best predictor of a nation's well-being wasn't the amount that the society spent on healthcare, education, or housing. It wasn't how rich the country was, either in aggregate or on average. It definitely wasn't how many millionaires or billionaires a country had.

Instead, they found that the countries with the greatest inequality in wealth and income had the absolute worst outcomes on a whole range of social and health measures, while the countries that had greater equality fared significantly, measurably better.

Every single index is worse in a country with great inequality. They include but are not limited to the following:

- Infant mortality
- Life expectancy
- Depression and mental illness
- Height
- Birth weight
- The rate of teenage pregnancies
- Imprisonment rates
- Obesity
- Social mobility
- Children's educational performance
- Social and political trust and engagement
- Hypertension and heart disease
- Homicide and suicide

Looking at countries in the developed world, Pickett and Wilkinson found that the more unequal a nation was, the worse its outcomes.

They found that in the most unequal countries, mental illness rates were three times higher than in the most equal societies; people were 10 times more likely to end up in prison in the most unequal countries and three times more likely to be obese.

In 1980, when Ronald Reagan cut a deal with the Iranians to humiliate President Jimmy Carter and ended up president as a result,[3] America was a far more equal society. We had no billionaires, and average working people had job security and old-age security; it was even possible to live comfortably (albeit frugally) on Social Security prior to Reagan's 1983 "reforms."

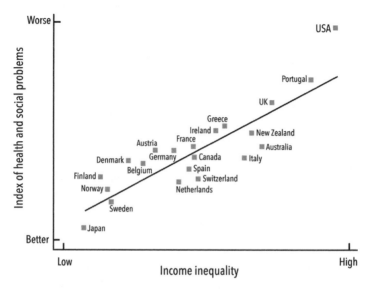

Health and social problems are closely related to inequality within rich countries.
Source: Wilkinson and Pickett, *The Spirit Level* (2009).[2]

Forty years of neoliberal Reaganomics have shredded that, making the United States the most unequal society in the developed world.

Data compiled by the Pew Research Center shows that the very rich went from having 29 percent of all the income in America in 1970 to 48 percent of all income in 2018. This small slice of the top few percent of Americans went from owning 60 percent of the entire nation's wealth in 1983 to having nailed down fully 79 percent of everything of value in 2018.

Meanwhile, working people went from having 62 percent of all income in America in 1970 to only getting 43 percent in 2018, and from owning 32 percent of wealth in the country in 1983 to a mere 17 percent in 2018.[4]

As a result, Wilkinson and Pickett pointed out, "in the United States during the period since 1980, when income inequality increased particularly rapidly . . . public expenditure on prisons increased six times as fast as public expenditure on higher education."[5] By every measure of societal and personal well-being, America has suffered profoundly from this explosion of inequality.

Prior to Reaganomics, the top tax rate on the very wealthy was 74 percent, and there was a hefty estate tax on the superwealthy. Corporations during the 1950s, when I grew up, paid between a third and half of the entire tax load that built the nation; today it's 13 percent.[6] When I went off to first grade in 1956, it was to a gleaming new school built with funds provided, in large part, by Republican president Dwight D. Eisenhower. We traveled on new highways, and when my younger brothers were born, they came into this world in new, state-of-the-art hospitals.

Throughout all my years in public school, I don't remember a single child with asthma or severe allergies and can remember only one "fat" kid—and he wasn't obese like we see today. I knew one person in high school who had to take insulin, and she had type 1 diabetes from childhood.

Ask any Americans in their late 60s or their 70s and they'll tell you the same story, pretty much regardless of where in the country they grew up. The "Reagan Revolution" truly was a revolution; it transformed this country.

We've come up with separate and individual solutions to the many and varied problems that Reagan's policies of inequality have brought the country. Longer jail terms for increased crime, SSRI drugs for childhood (and adult) depression, order-by-mail diet plans for obesity. And, of course, more—and more expensive—medical interventions for the many and varied illnesses that didn't seem to be much of a problem 40 years ago.

Yet all of these problems can be reduced, and the general physical, mental, and emotional health of America dramatically improved, by simply reducing income and wealth inequality—by just raising taxes on very rich people and big corporations back to levels we had before the Reagan Revolution.

A majority of the developed countries in the world have taken the path to greater equality, although the United States and the United Kingdom, suffering under the twin Reagan and Thatcher "revolutions," continue to slide into greater and greater inequality.

As Wilkinson and Pickett declared, "Politicians have an opportunity to do genuine good."[7]

Buy the Insurance Companies!

The biggest challenge to Medicare for All is lobbying of elected officials by health insurance companies. The industry, which makes hundreds of billions in profits and salaries every year, peels off a paltry few million every month or so to hand out to politicians across the nation.

Most contributions go to members of the US House of Representatives and Senate, although the industry lobbies in every state in the union, and lobbying expenses explode within states when they consider statewide single-payer plans, as Vermont and California have both done in recent years.

Add to this several million dollars every year that the industry spends to support anti-single-payer "think tanks" that produce an unending stream of policy papers, books, websites, Wikipedia edits, articles placed in local and national newspapers and magazines, and guest appearances on radio and TV.

It's really rather astonishing. An investment of a few hundred million dollars, spent carefully buying politicians and front groups who can be relied on to fight and block reform, produces trillions of dollars of revenue and hundreds of billions in profits every year.

Insurance companies, hospitals, and drug companies spend more money lobbying and doing PR than any other industry —even more than the defense and banking industries. The pharmaceutical industry spent $216 million in 2018, insurance $121 million, and hospitals and nursing homes $74 million.[8]

While a few hundred million dollars a year is chump change to big insurance companies, it's an overwhelming mountain to small, grassroots groups like Physicians for a National Health Program (PNHP), one of the most prominent and credible advocates for Medicare for All: their entire budget for *all* activities in 2018 was less than $1 million.[9]

Thus, every time there's been a serious effort to take on the big insurance companies, dating all the way back to Harry Truman's 1948 effort to put a single-payer program into place, the insurance companies simply steamroll the grassroots advocates.

It's a virtual certainty that no movement to push America into Medicare for All could raise over $100 million a year to lobby politicians and pay for a massive nationwide PR effort, which is why these efforts have failed for more than 70 years—even though polls have consistently shown that the majority of Americans favor a cheaper, more efficient, and more inclusive system.

So, what if we simply bought the companies to put a stop to all this corrupt activity?

The 10 largest publicly traded health insurance companies in America have a market capitalization—the price for which all of their stock could be purchased—of around $525 billion:

1. UnitedHealth Group (NYSE:UNH)—$235 billion
2. Anthem (NYSE:ANTM)—$73 billion
3. CVS Health (NYSE:CVS)—$72 billion
4. Cigna (NYSE:CI)—$61 billion
5. Humana (NYSE:HUM)—$36 billion
6. Centene (NYSE:CNC)—$21 billion
7. Wellcare Health Plans (NYSE:WCG)—$14 billion
8. Molina Healthcare (NYSE:MOH)—$9 billion
9. Magellan Health (NASDAQ:MGLN)—$1.7 billion
10. Health Insurance Innovations (NASDAQ: BFYT)—$348 million[10]

If the US government were to offer a 20 percent or slightly higher premium to induce shareholders to profitably part with their stock (something often done in mergers and acquisitions), virtually the entire sector could be picked up for under $700 billion. Add in the large players that aren't publicly traded, and you might push it to $1 trillion.

That's less than the United States *overpays* every year because of our for-profit system.

If we bought all of these companies, shut them down, and moved their productive workers who handle claims and sign people up over to a Medicare for All system, we'd recover the cost of buying them out in, at worst, two years.

Sure, there are a few dozen CEOs and a few hundred senior executives who'd have to retire with their many millions (or find other work), and shareholders would have to find other companies to bet on in the stock market, but tens of thousands of American lives would be saved every year, and the country overall would save trillions.

Medicare for All: The Losers

Under a Medicare for All system, there would be some losers.

Health insurance companies, for example, would shrink dramatically to serve only very wealthy people interested in gold-plated plans that covered everything from cosmetic surgery to international travel problems, much as they do in most other developed nations.

Senator Bernie Sanders's plan, for example, sets aside 1 percent of total health spending to help unemployed former insurance industry employees train for and find new jobs.

Drug companies right now are charging Americans massively more than citizens of any other developed countries in the world; that would come to an end when the government could assert bulk purchasing and competitive bidding, like every other developed country in the world. Big Pharma would have to reduce their dividend payments to stockholders, and their share prices might fall, reducing somewhat the multimillion-dollar annual compensation to their CEOs and senior executives.

Because the vast majority of new drug research in the United States is government funded, it's unlikely that this plan would have any impact whatsoever on the development of new medications; it's already an internationally competitive market, in any case. If we don't develop a drug in the United States, a company in India or China or Germany almost certainly will.

Doctors in the United States are wildly overpaid compared with the rest of the world—and, for that matter, compared with physician compensation in this country just a few generations ago. Growing up in a middle-class neighborhood in the 1950s, I played with one kid whose father was a dentist and another whose dad was a pediatrician, and we all lived in a neighborhood of $15,000 (1956 dollars) houses. Today, dentists and doctors are more likely to live in mansions in gated communities.

Hospital empires would find Medicare for All a mixed blessing. On the one hand, their administrative and paperwork expenses would drop dramatically. A large hospital in the United States often has dozens or more people employed to bill, track, and collect payments, sometimes taking up an entire floor; a similar-size hospital in Canada or any other developed country dealing mostly with one single (government) payer gets the same work done by a small handful of people typically sharing one or two small offices.

American hospitals would see substantial savings from uncollectable billings for people who were indigent, uninsured, or simply unable to handle copays and other expenses that would all vanish under a Medicare for All system.

On the other hand, hospitals would now have to deal with a (government) single payer with so much market leverage that the hospitals would no longer be able to get away with charging $25 for two Tylenols, $18,000 for a bottle of baby formula and a room for an hour to feed the baby, and $6,000 for an ice pack and bandage handed to an injured person in an ER.[11]

The Impact of Medicare for All on Business

Late in 2004, Toyota announced that they were going to build a new factory in North America to meet demand for their cars. Several states invested millions of dollars in putting together sophisticated pitches to Toyota, offering the company free land and massive property and income tax breaks worth hundreds of millions.

In the end, in June 2005, the company announced that they were going to put the factory in Ontario, Canada, which had offered nothing even close to the US states in terms of incentives. The reason they chose Canada was simple: healthcare costs.[12]

Gary Cowger, who in 2004 was president of General Motors Corp.'s North American operations, told an audience of car dealers in 2004 that GM was spending $4.5 billion a year to cover the healthcare costs of their 1.2 million employees, retirees, and spouses.

"That's more than we spend on steel," he said. "It adds $1,200 to the cost of each GM vehicle."[13]

Medicare for All would make American manufacturing again competitive with the rest of the world.

It would also encourage entrepreneurism, the historical key to the vibrancy of American business. Our for-profit healthcare system has driven the cost of getting sick or injured up so high that many Americans are no longer willing to take the chance of leaving a job with healthcare benefits for the nakedness of starting up a small business on a shoestring.

Small businesses similarly would find existing and competing—particularly with larger companies—much easier when insurance didn't suck up "more than we spend on steel."

Finally, a whole variety of hidden healthcare expenses that hit small and medium-sized businesses particularly hard would vanish: workers' compensation insurance, the health riders in liability insurance, the health riders in auto and truck insurance, etc. Once everybody's in the same pool, all this fragmentation becomes unnecessary.

Want a Green New Deal? Get Medicare for All First

One of the things that people who live in countries with universal, taxpayer-funded healthcare coverage (all of the developed countries in the world except the United States) know, which Americans generally don't, is that anything that increases sickness or death among the general population also increases their taxes.

Conversely, as healthcare expenses go down, so do taxes (or that money can be used for other needs).

Danes, for example, know this well.

A decade or so ago, I was doing my radio show from Copenhagen, interviewing various Danish politicians and public figures—most of them calling themselves "conservatives."

If it's happening in Danish politics (or, for that matter, Scandinavian or European politics), Peter Mogensen knows about it.

An economist by training, he's the chief political editor of Denmark's second-largest national newspaper, *Politiken*, and for four years (1997–2000) he was the right-hand man (head of office and political adviser) to Denmark's prime minister from 1993 to 2001, Poul Nyrup Rasmussen. A handsome man of young middle years, he also plays in a Bruce Springsteen look-alike rock band and cuts a wide swath through Danish popular society.

So it was particularly interesting to see this normally unflappable man with a slightly confused look on his face.

We were in the studios of Danish Radio (their equivalent of BBC or NPR) in downtown Copenhagen, where I was broadcasting for a week in June 2008, and I'd just asked him how many Danes experienced financial distress, lost their homes, or even had to declare bankruptcy because of a major illness in the family.[14]

"Why, of course," he blinked a few times, "none."

I explained how every year in the United States, millions of families lose their jobs and their homes, and most of their most precious possessions are sold to satisfy the demands of creditors because they can't afford to pay the copays, deductibles, and expenses associated with having cancer, heart disease, auto accident injuries, or other serious conditions.

"Over half of all the bankruptcies in America," I told him on the air, "are because people can't afford these expenses, and their insurance companies don't cover all their expenses or they don't have health insurance."

He shook his head sadly. "Here in Denmark, we could not imagine living like that," he said.

Danish Radio later sponsored an online Q&A chat with me and their listeners.

"What makes you think we're so happy?" one woman asked, referencing Denmark having been credited for having the "happiest people in the world" that year. "Why aren't Americans just as happy as I am?"

I replied, "Can you imagine waking up every morning knowing that if you or your spouse or child was diagnosed that day with cancer or got in a car accident or had some other major injury, it could lead to your being bankrupt, homeless, and a pauper for the rest of your life?"

"Of course not. That's stupid," she replied dismissively.

"No," I said. "That's the reality for Americans."

"Impossible!" she said. "There would be a revolution! People in America would not stand for such a thing!"

After several similar, disbelieving callers, a young man called in to say that he'd been an exchange student who spent half a year in the United States and that, in fact, the situation I described was accurate. The Danes were astounded.

A day or two later, I had one of the city officials from Copenhagen on the show and asked about the recent program to convert a large number of the city's streets into wide bike lanes. He pointed out that the healthier people became because they biked to work every day, the less their healthcare would cost the city or the nation.

Another politician told me how Denmark had launched a national antismoking program, something he observed was common across European countries. The cost of the program, he said, would be recovered in less than two or three years because of the reduced healthcare costs when people took the campaign to heart and quit smoking.

Which ties together healthcare reform with Green New Deal–type reforms that decrease air pollution and the use of the fossil fuels that cause so much of it.

In 2020 testimony before the House Committee on Oversight and Reform, Michael Greenstone of the University of Chicago explained recent improvements in the ability to measure the health impacts of air pollution.

"The economic costs of climate-induced health risks," Greenstone testified, "are at least an order of magnitude larger than has previously been understood."[15]

He said that with emissions at their current rate, the number of people dying from air-pollution and climate-related causes (from diseases caused by inhaling air pollution to deaths from wildfires and extreme weather events) "is almost as large as the current fatality rate from cancers."

Drew Shindell, Distinguished Professor of Earth Sciences at Duke University, testified at the same hearing that following a Green New Deal–like plan, "[o]ver the next 50 years, keeping to the 2°C pathway would prevent roughly 4.5 million premature deaths, about 3.5 million hospitalizations and emergency room visits, and approximately 300 million lost workdays in the US."[16]

To put that in context, Representative Robin Kelly responded, "That's a huge number. That's nearly three times the number of lives we lose in car accidents every year. It's twice the number of deaths caused by opioids in the past few years."[17]

Shindell agreed and added, "The avoided deaths are valued at more than $37 trillion. The avoided healthcare spending due to reduced hospitalizations and emergency room visits exceeds $37 billion, and the increased labor productivity is valued at more than $75 billion."

Thus, he said, "[o]n average, this amounts to over $700 billion per year in benefits to the US from improved health and labor alone, far more than the cost of the energy transition."

In other words, the costs to America—both from air pollution associated with fossil fuels and from the damage being done to our nation by climate change—are so great that they'll burden our overall economy and also raise our healthcare expenses on an ongoing basis.

Right now, Americans don't see or understand any relationship between carbon pollution and the cost of their healthcare or their taxes. But if there were a single-payer type of system in the United States where we all knew what we were spending every year, the costs of fossil fuel pollution would show up as an identifiable number as part of our annual healthcare expense.

As would obesity and food deserts; poisonous fly ash and other waste from coal-fired power plants; crises like the water system in Flint, Michigan; and the high rates of disease experienced by people who live in "sacrifice zones" like the "cancer alley" 200-mile corridor downwind from Texas's and Louisiana's refineries.

The experience of other nations with single-payer systems shows that just instituting such a program alone becomes a big motivator for fossil fuel mitigation strategies, from carbon taxes to cleaning up industry to a Green New Deal.

PAYING FOR MEDICARE FOR ALL

You'd think that the first and major goal of a healthcare system would be to provide the *best healthcare* to the *most people* at the *lowest cost*. But in the United States, because healthcare has been treated as a commodity to be sold rather than a basic human right, we have the *worst* healthcare in the developed world, available to the *smallest* percentage of the population, at the *greatest* expense.

On the other hand, like any product marketed and sold as a commodity, healthcare in the United States produces enormous profits. It's the only measurable "upside" of our system, and one that inures only to the benefit of a handful of investors, executives, and physicians.

Every other developed country in the world has figured out how stupid and destructive this is for the majority of their citizens and fixed it. We haven't here, in large part because money plays such a large role in governance in America.

If that obstacle can be overcome—either through election and lobbying reform or through the brute force of public outrage amid a pandemic—the most efficient and cost-effective way to deliver healthcare is through a single-payer system, a variation of which is at the core of most developed countries' systems and already exists here as Medicare and Medicaid.

(We also have a socialist form of healthcare system, much like the UK's National Health Service, where the hospitals are owned by the government, and the doctors, nurses, and other staff are all government employees, but we limit this to the military.)

Expanding our largest and most popular existing single-payer system, Medicare, is the easiest way to get quality, inexpensive care to all Americans. But there are a few steps to get there.

The US government spends around $1.6 trillion a year on healthcare (Medicare, Medicaid, SSDI, military), while the private insurance industry extracts an additional $1.3 trillion a year from us and our employers. Medicaid picks up another $600 billion, and Americans pay about $400 billion every year out of pocket. Other parts of our healthcare system (workers' compensation, auto-based insurance covering collision injuries, etc.) spend around $570 billion a year.[18]

If we swept aside all the various and inefficient ways we pay for healthcare, and removed the hundreds of billions a year we give to executives and shareholders in insurance companies, Medicare for All would be estimated to cost around $3 trillion a year, an amount that roughly equals the combined cost of government spending and private insurance, leaving $1.57 trillion to build hospitals, train more doctors and nurses, and administer public health programs to deal with everything from our obesity crisis to pandemics.

The majority of Americans (around 157 million) get their healthcare coverage from a private plan paid for (all or in part) by the employer of a member of their family. This coverage is scattered across scores of for-profit insurance companies, HMOs, PPOs, and large employers who self-insure but have their payments administered by an insurance company.

Medicare, with 54 million people over 65 signed up (and a much smaller number of people under 65 with disabilities), is number two. Right behind that are Medicaid and the Children's Health Insurance Program (CHIP, funded through Medicaid), totaling 44 million recipients.

To expand our nation's existing single-payer system, Medicare, and have it cover everybody in the country, would involve just a few straightforward steps:

- Increase Medicare coverage for all current (over 65) Medicare recipients from 80 percent of expenses to a full 100 percent, eliminating the need for private Medigap coverage.

- Add dental, vision, hearing, and mental health services to round out coverage, and eliminate George W. Bush's ban on Medicare negotiating prescription drug prices.

- Replace the "over 65" part of the Medicare laws with "to all persons," as Senator Daniel Patrick Moynihan once suggested.

- Phase in the program over a few years (most plans suggest four years) to give time to staff up to cover all Americans.

- In the process, roll into this Medicare for All coverage all other nonmilitary healthcare coverage systems in the United States, eliminating the need for and expense of employer-based health insurance, healthcare riders on car and trip insurance, workers' compensation health provisions, the Federal Employees Health Benefits Program, Tricare, the under-65 disability benefits under Medicare, and the various forms that Medicaid and CHIP take across the nation when administered by states.

- Outlaw the phony Medicare Advantage scam, but allow private Medicare Supplement Insurance to lessen political opposition from wealthy people who want things like international transportation, private hospital suites, experimental treatments, and plastic surgery coverage.

Eliminate the multiple payers, the multimillionaire executives, the obscene nonnegotiated drug expenditures, and the regular dividend checks to shareholders, and America will save as much as 10 percent (depending on whose figures you use) of total healthcare spending every year. The challenge will be in paying for it.

And that's not because it'll be more expensive, but because most of the actual costs of health insurance are hidden.

Employers pay for health insurance for the majority of Americans, and because it's a tax-deductible expense for the companies, the cost of that insurance never shows up on a worker's tax statement.

Medicare and Medicaid in their current forms are paid for from tax revenue, but those taxes have been with us for three generations, so they're nearly invisible.

And the people who are dying from lack of decent coverage are largely lower income and poor, and their right to vote is blocked, particularly in red states, at a radically higher percentage than wealthier people, so their plight is easy for politicians to ignore. (In the 2016 election, according to the EconoFact Network, "The 48 percent voting participation rate for families in the lowest income category in 2016 was a bit more than half of the 86 percent rate for families in the highest income category."[19])

To pay for this, Senator Bernie Sanders's plan would do the following:

- Impose a 7.5 percent payroll tax on payroll costs exceeding $1 million, equal to an average of $4,500 per employee per year (generating $5.2 trillion over 10 years). Contrast that with the average $14,500 per year per employee that American companies pay for health insurance right now.

- Require individuals to pay a health insurance premium through a 4 percent payroll tax on all income over $29,000, representing $1,240 per year for the average American family of four. That average American family is *today* paying $6,015.

- Fill in the cracks by eliminating the tax deductibility of health insurance for corporations ($4.2 trillion/decade); having those with incomes over $250,000 a year "pay the same rate into Social Security as working families" and taxing dividends and capital gains as ordinary income ($2.5 trillion); and imposing a 1 percent wealth tax on every dollar of net worth above $32 million (estimated revenues/decade: $350 billion out of $4.35 trillion raised).[20]

- Close the "offshore profits" and "S-corp pass-through" income tax loopholes used by giant corporations and hedge funds ($1.2 trillion).

The plan that Democratic senator Elizabeth Warren of Massachusetts rolled out during the 2020 presidential election also pays for Medicare for All in a simple, straightforward way:[21]

- Eliminate massive administrative overhead costs from fat-cat compensation and multiple payers, and negotiate down obscene pharma costs.

- Employers pay about $20 billion a year *less* than what they are paying now for employee health insurance, but the money goes as taxes into a Medicare for All fund instead of to the insurance companies, their executives, and their shareholders. Companies under 50 employees don't pay anything.

- Properly fund the IRS (after three decades of slashed budgets and cut enforcement) so they can recover the roughly $700 billion a year that the top 5 percent of Americans avoid paying through scams, frauds, and outright nonpayment of taxes.

- Raise another $800 billion a year with a 0.1 percent tax (10 cents on every $100) on financial transactions. We had a tax like this (the securities transactions excise tax) from the 1930s to the 1960s, and it didn't negatively impact the economy in any meaningful way.

- End the ability of giant American-based corporations to avoid paying US income taxes on their huge profits by pretending they're actually Irish or Bahamian corporations.

- Impose a 0.1 percent wealth tax on all individual assets over $50 million. Most Americans already pay a much higher wealth tax on their main asset—their home. Property taxes vary from 2.35 percent in New Jersey to 0.27 percent in Hawaii, but in every case, middle-class homeowners across America pay a wealth tax on the value of their home every year.[22] This would simply tax billionaires' assets above $50 million the same way, but at a very low 0.1 percent rate.

- Tax annual income earned from investing (*capital gains*) at the same rate as income earned from working, similar to what Ronald Reagan proposed —and did for one year—back in the 1980s.

These changes in our tax code would not only pay for Medicare for All but also make our tax system somewhat less heavily skewed to the advantage of high-income people; the system would become fairer.

No matter which plan was adopted, the country would save money, every American would have access to top-notch healthcare at little or no cost as a right instead of a privilege, tens of thousands of lives would be saved every year, and a half million families would no longer go bankrupt every year because of healthcare costs.

"It Takes a Crisis"

During an October 5, 2020, nationally televised discussion of healthcare policy sponsored by Social Security Works, Representative Debbie Dingell of Michigan pointed out that her late father-in-law, Representative John Dingell Sr., had participated in pushing Social Security through Congress in the 1930s.

"It takes a crisis," she said;[23] the Republican Great Depression was such a shock to the American system that envisioning and enacting major systemic change became a reality.

Today, America is in the midst of a crisis that rivals the Republican Great Depression of the 1930s. Between 40 years of disastrous neoliberal Reaganomics policies and the coronavirus pandemic, people are hurting in ways never before seen by most living Americans.

Back in 2008, as the deregulation policies of George W. Bush provoked a full-out real estate and banking disaster, then-Representative Rahm Emanuel famously said, "You never want a serious crisis to go to waste. And what I mean by that is an opportunity to do things that you think you could not do before."[24]

There is broad agreement that public health is a core function of government, having evolved from the smallpox era of the Founding Generation through the typhoid fever and tuberculosis epidemics of the late 19th century to polio in the 20th century.

George Washington was the first US government official to mandate vaccination and to create a single-payer healthcare system specifically for sailors, both military and civilian. Individual states largely dealt with the epidemics of the 19th century and venereal diseases, but by the 20th century there was a consensus about the importance of a national approach to polio and other serious illnesses.

As the number of Americans infected with the coronavirus passed 25 million in early 2021, with large numbers of those people having to cope with medical bills as well as a potentially deadly disease, a new national consensus began to emerge.

Every other developed country in the world holds its healthcare system at the core of its public health system. We have a few rules about reporting and coordination, but by and large the United States is the outlier, as our healthcare system is so fragmented and sliced into various profit-making pieces.

Hopefully this pandemic will make clear to all Americans the importance of a single, integrated, and fully functional national healthcare system.

NOTES

Introduction: How a Single-Payer Healthcare System Helped Stop COVID-19

1. https://www.usatoday.com/story/news/nation/2020/07/23/united-states-coronavirus-cases-deaths-timeline/5485674002/

2. https://thediplomat.com/2020/09/taiwans-covid-19-success-story-continues-as-neighbors-fend-off-new-outbreaks/

3. https://www.vox.com/health-care/2020/1/13/21028702/medicare-for-all-taiwan-health-insurance

4. This is a conservative number. The *British Medical Journal* documents 26,000 Americans dying every year from lack of a national healthcare system. Multiply that by the number of years since 1945 and decrease the total somewhat to account for lower overall population numbers in decades past, and then raise the number somewhat to account for all the years before the 1960s when Medicare and Medicaid were put into place, and it will be multiples of the number of US deaths in World War II. https://www.ncbi.nlm.nih.gov/pmc/articles/PMC2323087/.

5. David U. Himmelstein, MD, et al., *Medical Bankruptcy: Still Common Despite the Affordable Care Act* (Washington, DC: American Public Health Association, 2019), https://ajph.aphapublications.org/doi/10.2105/AJPH.2018.304901.

6. Martin Gaynor, Farzad Mostashari, and Paul B. Ginsburg, "Making Health Care Markets Work: Competition Policy for Healthcare," Center for Health Policy at Brookings, April 2017, https://www.brookings.edu/wp-content/uploads/2017/04/gaynor-et-al-final-report-v11.pdf.

7. https://www.scribd.com/document/129257573/How-to-Think-Clearly-About-Medicare

8. https://www.healthaffairs.org/doi/10.1377/hlthaff.2009.0075

9. Kurt Andersen, *Evil Geniuses: The Unmaking of America* (New York: Random House, 2020), 233.

10. https://www.forbes.com/sites/adamandrzejewski/2019/06/26/top-u-s-non-profit-hospitals-ceos-are-racking-up-huge-profits/?sh=34aae24719df

11. https://www.pbs.org/newshour/health/health-costs-how-the-us-compares-with-other-countries

12. https://www.ahip.org/wp-content/uploads/IB_StateofMedigap2019.pdf

13. https://www.healthline.com/health/medicare/medicare-eligibility-disability#help-with-costs
14. https://www.jhsph.edu/news/news-releases/2019/us-health-care-spending-highest-among-developed-countries.html
15. https://jamanetwork.com/journals/jama/article-abstract/2674671
16. Ibid.
17. Ibid.
18. https://www.nytimes.com/2021/02/18/us/covid-life-expectancy.html
19. https://www.ced.org/pdf/Economic_Contribution_of_the_Food_and_Beverage_Industry.pdfs

Part One: How Bad Things Are in America

1. https://www.opensecrets.org/members-of-congress/industries?cid=N00000616&cycle=Career
2. https://www.thedailybeast.com/traitor-joe
3. https://www.nytimes.com/2000/08/08/us/the-2000-campaign-the-record-senator-often-stands-to-right-of-his-party.html
4. *Buckley v. Valeo*, in 1976, legalized political bribery by very wealthy individuals. In 1978, conservatives on the Court expanded that "right" to corporations. In 2010, they expanded both provisions with their conservative-votes-only *Citizens United v. Federal Election Commission* decision.
5. https://www.heritage.org/social-security/report/assuring-affordable-health-care-all-americans
6. https://www.npr.org/sections/itsallpolitics/2015/10/23/451200436/mitt-romney-finally-takes-credit-for-obamacare
7. https://www.politifact.com/factchecks/2009/jul/16/barack-obama/obama-statements-single-payer-have-changed-bit/
8. https://www.politico.com/blogs/ben-smith/2009/06/obama-rejects-single-payer-019106
9. https://publicintegrity.org/health/elimination-of-public-option-threw-consumers-to-the-insurance-wolves/
10. Ibid.
11. Ibid.
12. Wendell Potter, *Deadly Spin: An Insurance Company Insider Speaks Out on How Corporate PR Is Killing Health Care and Deceiving Americans* (New York: Bloomsbury Press, 2010).
13. https://news.harvard.edu/gazette/story/2009/09/new-study-finds-45000-deaths-annually-linked-to-lack-of-health-coverage/

14. https://www.startribune.com/mcguire-s-payday-is-a-shame-if-not-a-crime/11093081

15. Charles Forelle and James Bandler, "The Perfect Payday: Some CEOs Reap Millions by Landing Stock Options When They Are Most Valuable. Luck—or Something Else?" *Wall Street Journal*, March 18, 2006, https://www.wsj.com/articles/SB114265075068802118.

16. Lewis Krauskopf and Martha Graybow, "Ex-UnitedHealth CEO McGuire to Forfeit Over $400 Million," Reuters, December 6, 2007, https://www.reuters.com/article/us-unitedhealth-1-idUSKUA68488720071206.

17. Fred Schulte, "UnitedHealth Doctored Medicare Records, Overbilled U.S. by $1 Billion, Feds Claim," Kaiser Health News, May 17, 2017, https://khn.org/news/unitedhealth-doctored-medicare-records-overbilled-u-s-by-1-billion-feds-claim/.

18. Matt Stieb, "Rick Scott's Company Committed Historic Medicare Fraud. He Will Now Lead Trump's Health-Care Push," *Intelligencer*, April 1, 2019, https://nymag.com/intelligencer/2019/04/rick-scott-is-an-odd-choice-to-lead-gops-health-care-reform.html.

19. https://khn.org/news/unitedhealth-doctored-medicare-records-overbilled-u-s-by-1-billion-feds-claim/

20. https://publicintegrity.org/topics/health/medicare-advantage-money-grabs

21. Ibid.

22. https://publicintegrity.org/health/health-insurers-have-their-way-with-regulators/

23. https://www.brown.senate.gov/newsroom/press/release/brown-colleagues-urge-cms-to-investigate-medicare-advantage-overbilling-protect-taxpayer-dollars-and-improve-care-for-older-ohioans

24. https://www.nytimes.com/2020/02/21/business/medicare-advantage-retirement.html

25. https://www.nber.org/system/files/working_papers/w23090/w23090.pdf

26. https://www.cancer.org/cancer/prostate-cancer/about/key-statistics.html

27. https://www.statnews.com/2018/01/17/medicare-cuts-improvement/

28. https://www.nytimes.com/2020/02/21/business/medicare-advantage-retirement.html

29. http://realkochfacts.com/rick-scott-the-special-interests-governor/

30. https://www.theguardian.com/us-news/2018/feb/11/paid-sick-leave-koch-brothers-nfib

31. http://www.tampabay.com/opinion/columns/column-the-price-of-ideology-a-womans-life/2174497

32. http://mywomenonthemove.com/a-casualty-of-rick-scott-the-florida-legislature-and-the-party-of-no/

33. https://www.floridadems.org/news/rick-scott-the-ultimate-medicare-thief

34. https://www.politifact.com/factchecks/2014/mar/03/florida-democratic-party/rick-scott-rick-scott-oversaw-largest-medicare-fra/

35. https://www.tampabay.com/opinion/columns/column-the-price-of-ideology-a-womans-life/2174497/

36. https://www.dailykos.com/stories/2014/4/19/1293155/-Death-by-Dogma-Charlene-Dill-Didn-t-Have-to-Die

37. https://publicpolicy.pepperdine.edu/academics/research/faculty-research/new-deal/roosevelt-speeches/fr092332.htm

38. https://www.nlm.nih.gov/exhibition/phs_history/seamen.html

39. https://www.ssa.gov/history/witte4.html

40. http://www.fdrlibrary.marist.edu/daybyday/event/january-1945-10/

41. https://www.trumanlibrary.gov/library/public-papers/128/special-message-congress-presenting-21-point-program-reconversion-period

Part Two: The Origins of America's Sickness-for-Profit System

1. https://www.history.com/topics/germany/karl-marx

2. https://www.thegreatcoursesdaily.com/what-happened-to-marxism-in-germany-after-marx/

3. https://fellowamericandaily.com/obamacare-found-to-violate-rights-of-the-people/

4. http://germanhistorydocs.ghi-dc.org/pdf/eng/429_BismarckWorker's%20Comp_130.pdf

5. Ann-Louise Shapiro, "Private Rights, Public Interest, and Professional Jurisdiction: The French Public Health Law of 1902," *Bulletin of the History of Medicine* 54, no. 1 (Spring 1980): 4–22, https://www.jstor.org/stable/44441228?seq=1#metadata_info_tab_contents.

6. https://www.britannica.com/topic/social-insurance

7. https://www.cnbc.com/2020/01/21/41-percent-of-americans-would-be-able-to-cover-1000-dollar-emergency-with-savings.html

8. http://files.kff.org/attachment/report-2015-employer-health-benefits-survey

9. Beatrix Hoffman, "Scientific Racism, Insurance, and Opposition to the Welfare State: Frederick L. Hoffman's Transatlantic Journey," *Journal of the Gilded Age and Progressive Era* 2, no. 2 (2003): 150–90, accessed May 17, 2020, http://www.jstor.org/stable/25144326.

10. James S. Olson, *Bathsheba's Breast: Women, Cancer, and History* (Baltimore, MD: The Johns Hopkins University Press, 2002), 155.

11. Eugene R. Corson, *The Vital Equation of the Colored Race and Its Future in the United States* (Norderstedt, Germany: Hansebooks, 2019).

12. Georgia Historical Society, "Eugene Rollin Corson Family Papers, 1858–1948," http://ghs.galileo.usg.edu/ghs/view?docId=ead/MS%20 2142-ead.xml.

13. Herbert Spencer, "Theory of Population Deduced from the General Law of Animal Fertility," *Westminster Review*, LVII (1852): 468–501, cited by John S. Haller Jr., *Outcasts from Evolution: Scientific Attitudes of Racial Inferiority, 1859–1900* (Champaign, IL: University of Illinois Press, 1986, 1st ed.), 47–48.

14. Frederick L. Hoffman, *Race Traits and Tendencies of the American Negro* (New York: Macmillan Company, 1896).

15. Ibid., 31.

16. *New York Times*, "The Bradley Martin Fete: The Search for Heirlooms, All Outside Windows to Be Boarded Up—All Spare Rooms Secured," February 10, 1897, 7.

17. *New York Times*, "Some Crank Sends a Bomb: The Bradley Martins Have a Disagreeable Surprise," February 10, 1897.

18. Daniel T. Rodgers, *Atlantic Crossings: Social Politics in a Progressive Age* (Cambridge, MA: Belknap Press, 1998), 256.

19. Anne-Emanuelle Birn, ScD, Theodore M. Brown, PhD, Elizabeth Fee, PhD, and Walter J. Lear, MD, "Struggles for National Health Reform in the United States," *American Journal of Public Health* 93, no. 1 (January 2003): 86–91, https://www.ncbi.nlm.nih.gov/pmc/articles /PMC1447697/.

20. https://1752.com/

21. Hoffman, "Scientific Racism, Insurance, and Opposition to the Welfare State."

22. Hoffman.

23. Hoffman.

24. Daniel T. Rodgers, *Atlantic Crossings: Social Politics in a Progressive Age* (Cambridge, MA: Belknap Press, 1998), 256.

25. Hoffman, "Scientific Racism, Insurance, and Opposition to the Welfare State."

26. Frederick Ludwig Hoffman, *More Facts and Fallacies of Compulsory Health Insurance* (Miami, FL: HardPress, 2017, Kindle edition; orig. pub. Prudential Press, 1920).

27. Ibid.

28. "Bulletin No. 250 of the United States Bureau of Labor Statistics on 'Welfare Work for Employees in Industrial Establishments,'" Washington, DC, 1919, quoted in Frederick Ludwig Hoffman, *More Facts and Fallacies of Compulsory Health Insurance*, 60.

29. Hoffman, *More Facts and Fallacies of Compulsory Health Insurance*, 185.

30. John R. Commons, "Health Insurance," *Wisconsin Medical Journal* 17 (1918): 222; quoted in Numbers, *Almost Persuaded*, 78, quoted in Beatrix Hoffman, "Scientific Racism, Insurance, and Opposition to the Welfare State."

31. Hoffman, "Scientific Racism, Insurance, and Opposition to the Welfare State."

32. Hoffman.

33. Scott J. Paltrow, "Past Due: In Relic of '50s and '60s, Blacks Still Pay More for a Type of Insurance," *Wall Street Journal*, April 27, 2000, quoted in Beatrix Hoffman, "Scientific Racism, Insurance, and Opposition to the Welfare State."

Part Three: The Modern Fight for a Human Right to Healthcare

1. https://www.firerescue1.com/fire-products/administration-billing/articles/how-todays-public-fire-departments-were-born-from-private-fire-brigades-M240qcm83TewqNsx/

2. https://francesperkinscenter.org/life-new/

3. Ibid.

4. Ibid.

5. https://www.ssa.gov/history/perkinsradio.html

6. Ibid.

7. http://francesperkinscenter.org/wp-content/uploads/2014/04/July-2016-Newsletter-2.pdf

8. https://www.seattlepi.com/local/opinion/article/Nothing-to-fear-but-no-health-care-1297612.php

9. Quoted in Jaap Kooijman, "Soon or Later On: Franklin D. Roosevelt and National Health Insurance, 1933–1945," *Presidential Studies Quarterly* 29, no. 2 (1999): 336–50, accessed August 24, 2020, http://www.jstor.org/stable/27551992.

10. Ibid.

11. http://www.historyofwar.org/articles/weapons_USS_Augusta_CA31.html

12. https://www.politico.com/story/2017/08/09/churchill-fdr-meet-off-newfoundland-aug-9-1941-241372

13. Rex Stout, *The Illustrious Dunderheads* (New York: Alfred A. Knopf, 1942).

14. Ibid.

15. https://www.fdrlibrary.org/atlantic-charter

16. https://www.nato.int/cps/en/natohq/official_texts_16912.htm

17. https://www.politico.com/story/2017/08/09/churchill-fdr-meet-off-newfoundland-aug-9-1941-241372

18. https://cis.mit.edu/sites/default/files/documents/Elizabeth%20Borgwardt%20paper.pdf

19. National Resources Planning Board, "After the War—Toward Security: Freedom From Want," September 1942, FDRPL, PSF, Postwar Planning, Box 157, Introductory Note, 1, 8.

20. Cynthia Soohoo, Catherine Albisa, and Martha F. Davis, *Bringing Human Rights Home: A History of Human Rights in the United States* (Westport, CT: Praeger Publishers, 2008).

21. http://www.bbc.co.uk/history/ww2peopleswar/timeline/factfiles/nonflash/a1143578.shtml

22. https://www.sochealth.co.uk/national-health-service/public-health-and-wellbeing/beveridge-report/

23. https://beveridgefoundation.org/sir-william-beveridge/

24. *Welfare and the State: Critical Concepts in Political Science*, eds. Nicholas Deakin, Catherine Jones-Finer, and Bob Matthews, vol. 3, *Welfare States and Societies in the Making* (New York: Routledge, 2004), 232.

25. https://ww-article-cache-1.s3.amazonaws.com/en/Beveridge_Report

26. http://www.ibiblio.org/pha/policy/1943/1943-03-21a.html

27. https://www.historic-uk.com/HistoryUK/HistoryofBritain/Birth-of-the-NHS/

28. http://www.ibiblio.org/pha/policy/1943/1943-03-21a.html

29. https://www.bmj.com/rapid-response/2011/10/31/without-winston-churchill-nhs-would-not-exist

30. https://www.neatorama.com/2012/05/07/the-greatest-canadian/

31. Ibid.

32. https://www.nytimes.com/1983/02/15/science/health-care-in-canada-popular-system-now-rocked-by-criticism.html

33. https://www.neatorama.com/2012/05/07/the-greatest-canadian/

34. https://canadiandimension.com/articles/view/the-birth-of-medicare

35. Ibid.

36. Ibid.

37. Luke Savage, "Tommy Douglas, Canada's Great Prairie Socialist, Wasn't Always So Beloved," *Jacobin*, June 5, 2019, https://www.jacobinmag.com/2019/06/tommy-douglas-ndp-ccf-socialist-medicare.

38. https://newrepublic.com/article/122396/john-f-kennedy-medicare

39. https://www.americanrhetoric.com/speeches/ronaldreagansocialized medicine.htm

40. David Barton Smith, *The Power to Heal: Civil Rights, Medicare, and the Struggle to Transform America's Health Care System* (Nashville, TN: Vanderbilt University Press, 2016).

41. Robert Dallek, *Flawed Giant: Lyndon Johnson and His Times, 1961–1973* (New York: Oxford University Press, 1998), 210.

42. https://www.ama-assn.org/sites/ama-assn.org/files/corp/media-browser/public/ama-history/african-american-physicians-organized-medicine-timeline.pdf

43. Joseph A. Califano Jr., *The Triumph and Tragedy of Lyndon Johnson: The White House Years* (New York: Simon & Shuster, 1991), 50–51.

44. https://www.history.com/news/americans-once-avoided-the-hospital-at-all-costs-until-ers-changed-that

45. Smith, *The Power to Heal.*

46. https://www.ssa.gov/history/tally65.html

47. Smith, *The Power to Heal.*

48. Smith.

49. Smith.

50. https://www.nytimes.com/1964/06/19/archives/text-of-goldwater-speech-on-rights.html

51. https://www.cms.gov/About-CMS/Agency-Information/History/Downloads/CMSPresidentsSpeeches.pdf

52. Smith, *The Power to Heal.*

53. https://historynewsnetwork.org/article/131473

54. https://www.trumanlibrary.gov/library/public-papers/192/special-message-congress-recommending-comprehensive-health-program

Part Four: Saving Lives with a Real Healthcare System

1. The Equality Trust, 356 Holloway Road, London, UK N7 6PA, https://www.equalitytrust.org.uk/.

2. Richard Wilkinson and Kate Pickett, "Health and Social Problems Are Worse in More Unequal Countries," *The Spirit Level: Why Greater Equality Makes Societies Stronger* (London, UK: Penguin, 2009), accessed via Wikimediacommons.org, February 17, 2021.

3. https://www.csmonitor.com/Commentary/Global-Viewpoint/2013 / 0305/Argo-helps-Iran-s-dictatorship-harms-democracy

4. https://www.pewsocialtrends.org/2020/01/09/trends-in-income-and-wealth-inequality/

5. https://evonomics.com/wilkinson-pickett-income-inequality-fix-economy/

6. https://www.taxpolicycenter.org/statistics/amount-revenue-source

7. https://evonomics.com/wilkinson-pickett-income-inequality-fix-economy/

8. https://www.opensecrets.org/industries/lobbying.php?cycle= 2020&ind=H03

9. https://www.influencewatch.org/non-profit/physicians-for-a-national-health-program-pnhp/

10. https://www.fool.com/investing/10-biggest-health-insurance-stocks.aspx

11. https://www.healthline.com/health-news/80-percent-hospital-bills-have-errors-are-you-being-overcharged#Hidden-costs-of-care

12. https://www.nytimes.com/2005/07/25/opinion/toyota-moving-northward.html

13. https://www.wardsauto.com/news-analysis/gm-getting-sick-high-health-care-costs

14. June 23–27, 2008, was the week I did my show from Copenhagen.

15. https://epic.uchicago.edu/news/michael-greenstone-testifies-on-the-devastating-health-impacts-of-climate-change/

16. https://oversight.house.gov/sites/democrats.oversight.house.gov /files/Testimony%20Shindell.pdf

17. https://oversight.house.gov/news/press-releases/oversight-committee-and-top-experts-examine-new-data-on-the-health-and-economic

18. All 2019 numbers, https://www.nytimes.com/interactive/2019/04/10 /upshot/medicare-for-all-bernie-sanders-cost-estimates.html.

19. https://econofact.org/voting-and-income

20. https://www.moneycrashers.com/medicare-for-all-features-costs/

21. https://elizabethwarren.com/plans/paying-for-m4a

22. https://www.usatoday.com/story/money/2019/05/20/property-taxes-state-which-has-highest-and-lowest/3697929002/

23. https://fb.watch/3I5MzRNTEq/

24. https://www.goodreads.com/quotes/717228-you-never-want-a-serious-crisis-to-go-to-waste

ACKNOWLEDGMENTS

Special thanks go to Troy N. Miller, who worked with me for years as a producer and writer for the television show *The Big Picture*, which I hosted every weeknight for seven years in Washington, DC. Troy worked hard as a researcher, sounding board, and editor, and deserves recognition for it.

At Berrett-Koehler Publishers, Steve Piersanti—who was the founder—worked with me to kick off this series. It's been a labor of love for both of us, and I'm so grateful to Steve for his insights, rigor, and passion for this project. Of the many other people at BK who have helped with this book (and some projects associated with it), special thanks to Jeevan Sivasubramaniam (who has helped keep me sane for years) and Neal Maillet, a constant source of encouragement and wisdom. BK is an extraordinary publishing company, and it's been an honor to have them publish my books for almost two decades. And thanks to Tai Moses, who edited my *Thom Hartmann Reader* and returned to do a first pass with this book, for all her insights and help.

BK also provided a brilliant final editor for the *Hidden History* book series, Elissa Rabellino, who did a great job smoothing and tightening the text.

Bill Gladstone, my agent for over two decades, helped make this book—and the *Hidden History* series—possible. Bill is truly one of the best in the business.

My executive producer, Shawn Taylor, helped with booking expert guests on my radio and TV programs, many of whom provided great information and anecdotes for this book. And my video producer, Nate Atwell, is a true visual genius. I'm blessed to have such a great team helping me produce a daily radio and TV program, which supports my writing work.

And, as always, my best sounding board, editor, and friend is my wife, Louise. Without her, in all probability none of my books would ever have seen the light of day.

INDEX

BOOKS BY THOM HARTMANN

Also in the Hidden History Series

The Hidden History of Monopolies

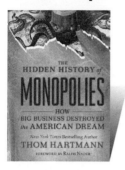

While it's well known that billionaire oligarchs and giant corporations have waged war against working-class Americans since the "Reagan Revolution," less well known is their war against small businesses. Robert Bork, a toxic Reagan acolyte, succeeded in transforming the nature and enforcement of America's anti-monopoly laws. The result is a shattered business landscape, the average family paying an annual $5,000 "monopoly tax" in higher prices for everything from airline flights to pharmaceuticals, and a massive increase in corporate political power. The coronavirus pandemic has only made things worse. The American business landscape—and the American middle class—will return to health only when Reaganism and Borkism are finally reversed.

Paperback, 192 pages, ISBN 978-1-5230-8773-0
PDF ebook, ISBN 978-1-5230-8774-7
ePub ebook, ISBN 978-1-5230-8775-4
Digital audio, ISBN 978-1-5230-8776-1

BK Berrett–Koehler Publishers, Inc.
www.bkconnection.com   **800.929.2929**

Berrett–Koehler
Publishers

Berrett-Koehler is an independent publisher dedicated to an ambitious mission: *Connecting people and ideas to create a world that works for all.*

Our publications span many formats, including print, digital, audio, and video. We also offer online resources, training, and gatherings. And we will continue expanding our products and services to advance our mission.

We believe that the solutions to the world's problems will come from all of us, working at all levels: in our society, in our organizations, and in our own lives. Our publications and resources offer pathways to creating a more just, equitable, and sustainable society. They help people make their organizations more humane, democratic, diverse, and effective (and we don't think there's any contradiction there). And they guide people in creating positive change in their own lives and aligning their personal practices with their aspirations for a better world.

And we strive to practice what we preach through what we call "The BK Way." At the core of this approach is *stewardship,* a deep sense of responsibility to administer the company for the benefit of all of our stakeholder groups, including authors, customers, employees, investors, service providers, sales partners, and the communities and environment around us. Everything we do is built around stewardship and our other core values of *quality, partnership, inclusion,* and *sustainability.*

This is why Berrett-Koehler is the first book publishing company to be both a B Corporation (a rigorous certification) and a benefit corporation (a for-profit legal status), which together require us to adhere to the highest standards for corporate, social, and environmental performance. And it is why we have instituted many pioneering practices (which you can learn about at www.bkconnection.com), including the Berrett-Koehler Constitution, the Bill of Rights and Responsibilities for BK Authors, and our unique Author Days.

We are grateful to our readers, authors, and other friends who are supporting our mission. We ask you to share with us examples of how BK publications and resources are making a difference in your lives, organizations, and communities at www.bkconnection.com/impact.

Dear reader,

Thank you for picking up this book and welcome to the worldwide BK community! You're joining a special group of people who have come together to create positive change in their lives, organizations, and communities.

What's BK all about?

Our mission is to connect people and ideas to create a world that works for all.

Why? Our communities, organizations, and lives get bogged down by old paradigms of self-interest, exclusion, hierarchy, and privilege. But we believe that can change. That's why we seek the leading experts on these challenges—and share their actionable ideas with you.

A welcome gift

To help you get started, we'd like to offer you a free copy of one of our bestselling ebooks:

www.bkconnection.com/welcome

When you claim your **free ebook,** you'll also be subscribed to our blog.

Our freshest insights

Access the best new tools and ideas for leaders at all levels on our blog at ideas.bkconnection.com.

Sincerely,

Your friends at Berrett-Koehler

Certified

Corporation

MIX
Paper from
responsible sources
FSC® C011935